High Shelf

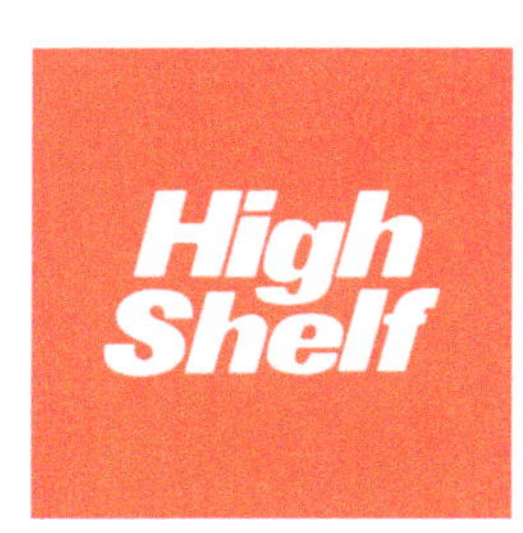

High Shelf XL. March 2022.
Portland, Oregon.
Copyright 2022, High Shelf Press

eBook ISBN: 978-1-952869-58-7

Cover Image by Min Ji Park
Editing, Design and Layout by C. M. Tollefson

With special thanks to:
David Seung & Eric Hoskins

High Shelf XL

March 2022

"... If to confess of time,
I have to speak in rivers with a face
lined with canyons, eyes sunken,

with a hand that grasps on nothing. ... "
Corinne Hughes

"... If only I had gathered you
into a pile of firm remembrances,
stones to mark the favored
plots from childhood

before they scattered like rocks

on the bottom of a riverbed, ..."
Jodie West

Table Of Contents

THE HORSE'S MOUTH

Roger Craik

"Love and marriage, love and marriage,
go together like a horse and carriage."

Of course. Just ask the horse.

Kill Joy

Sydney Yount

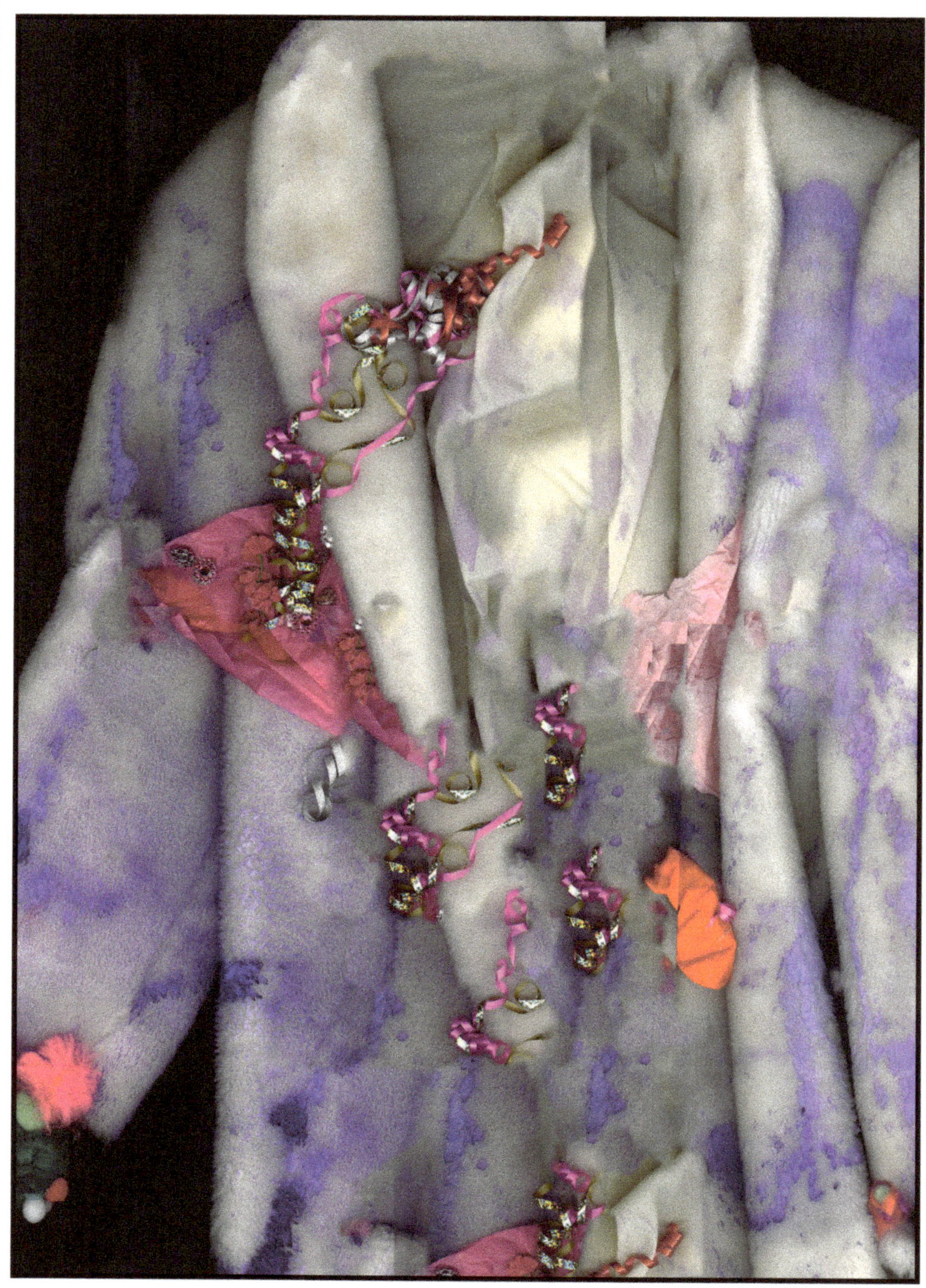

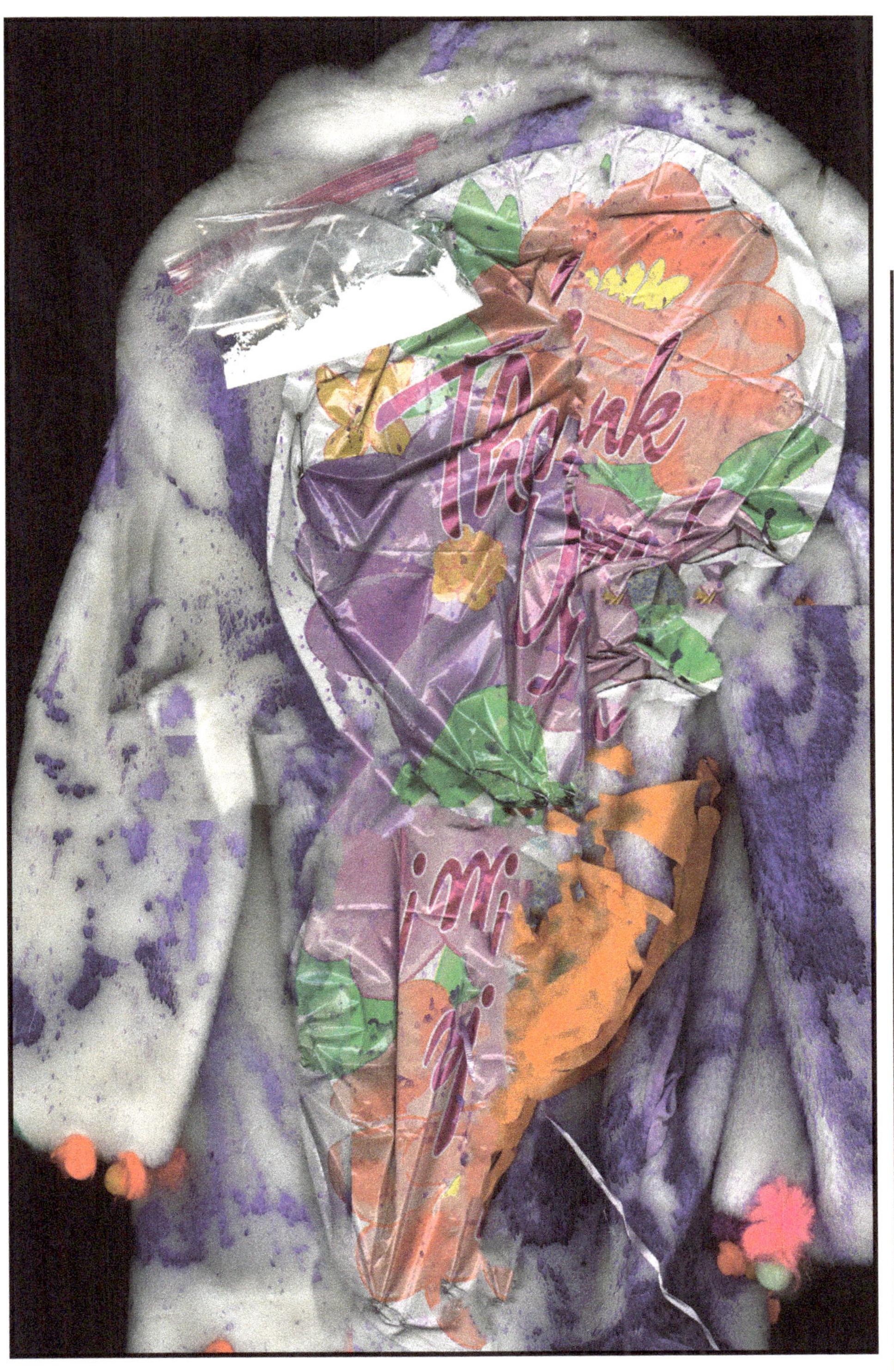

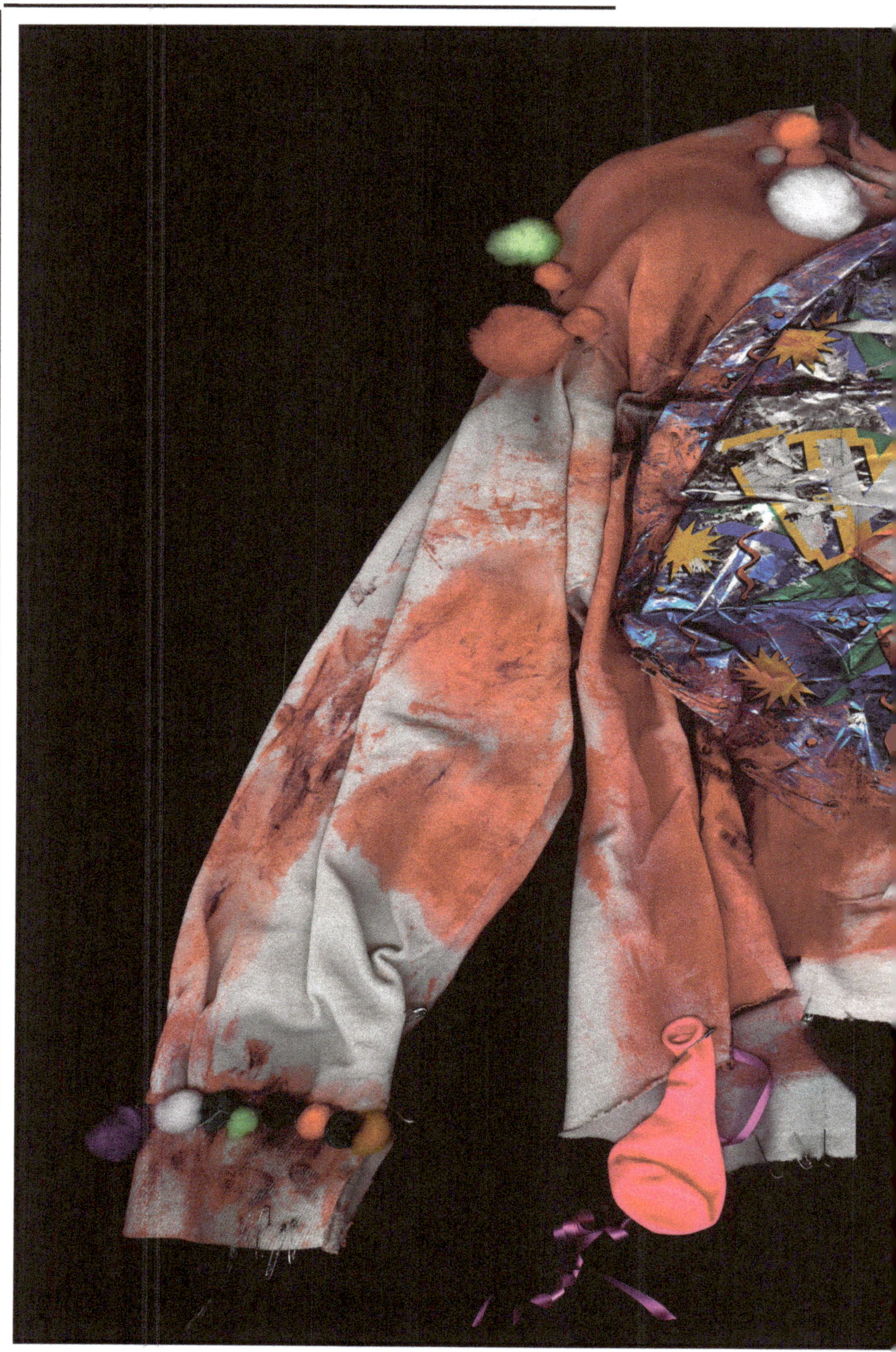

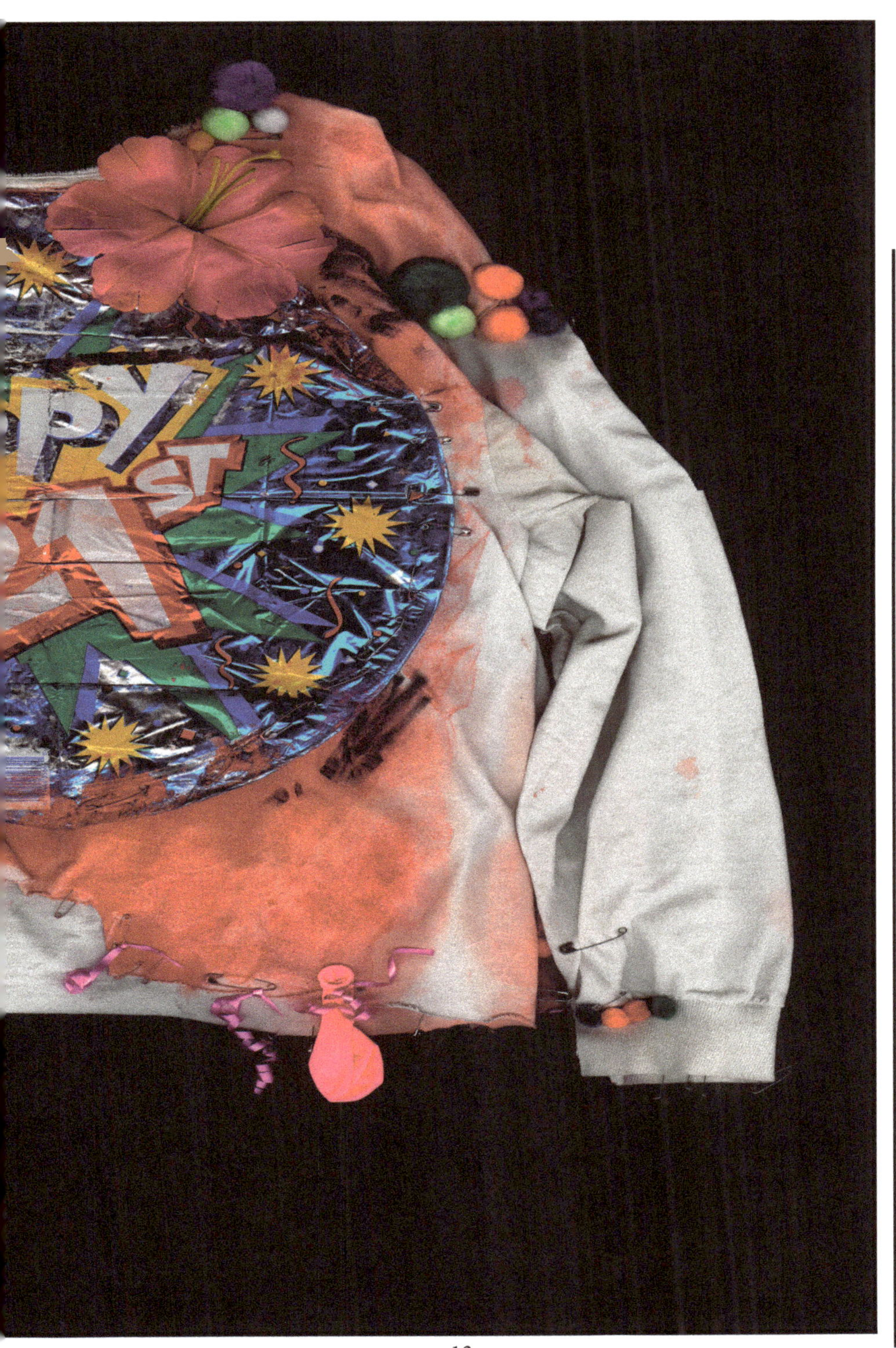

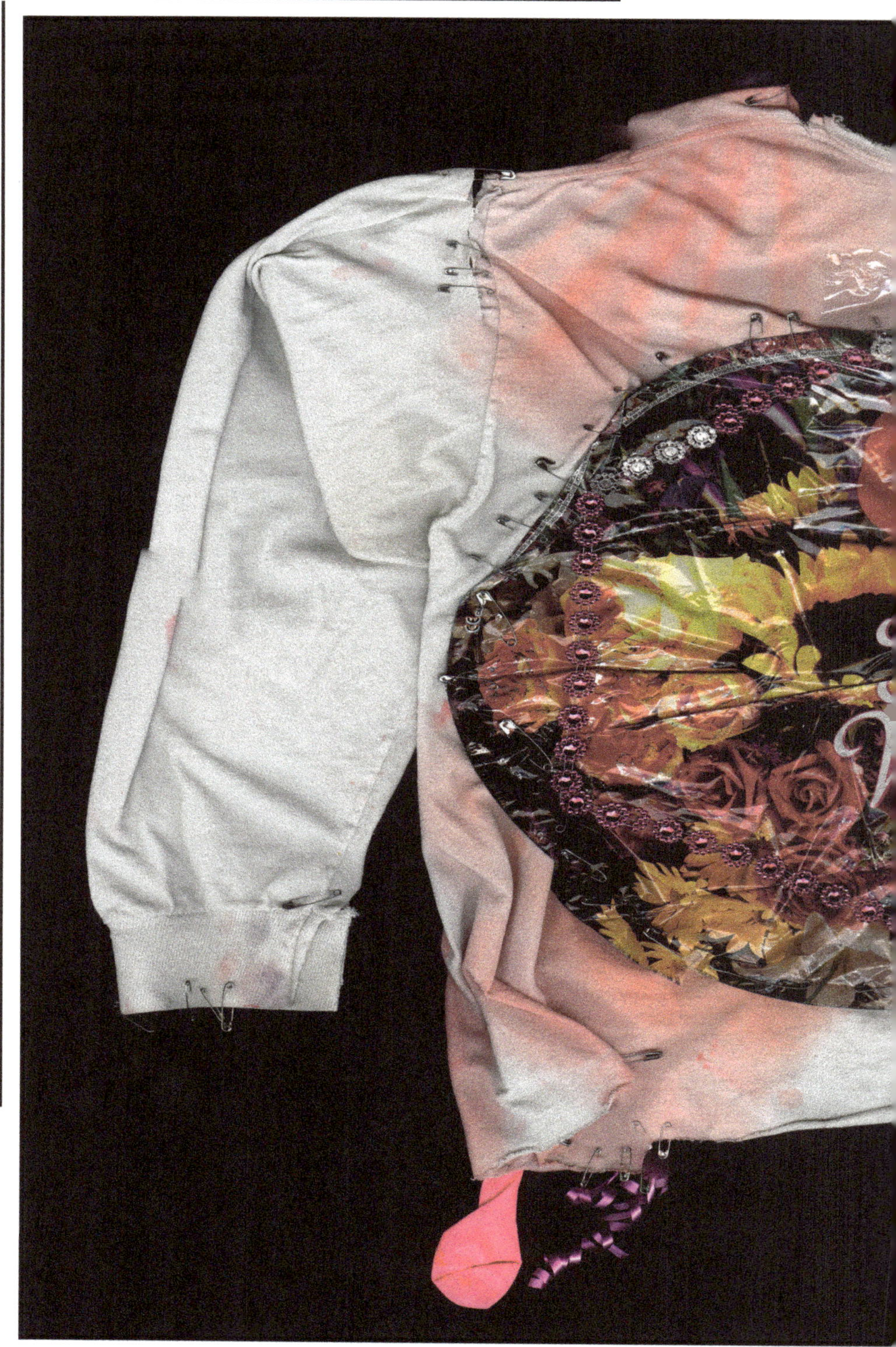

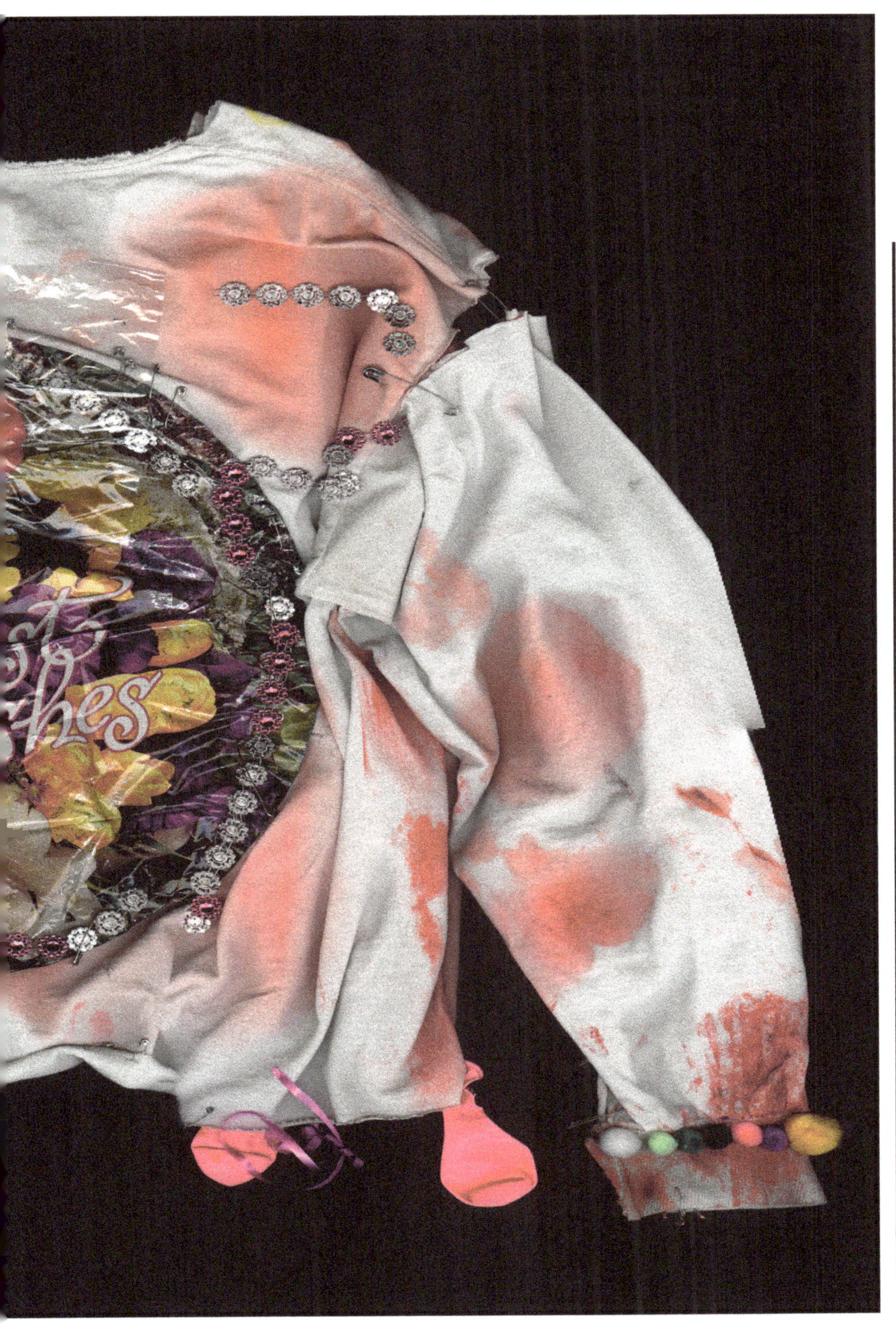
st
hes

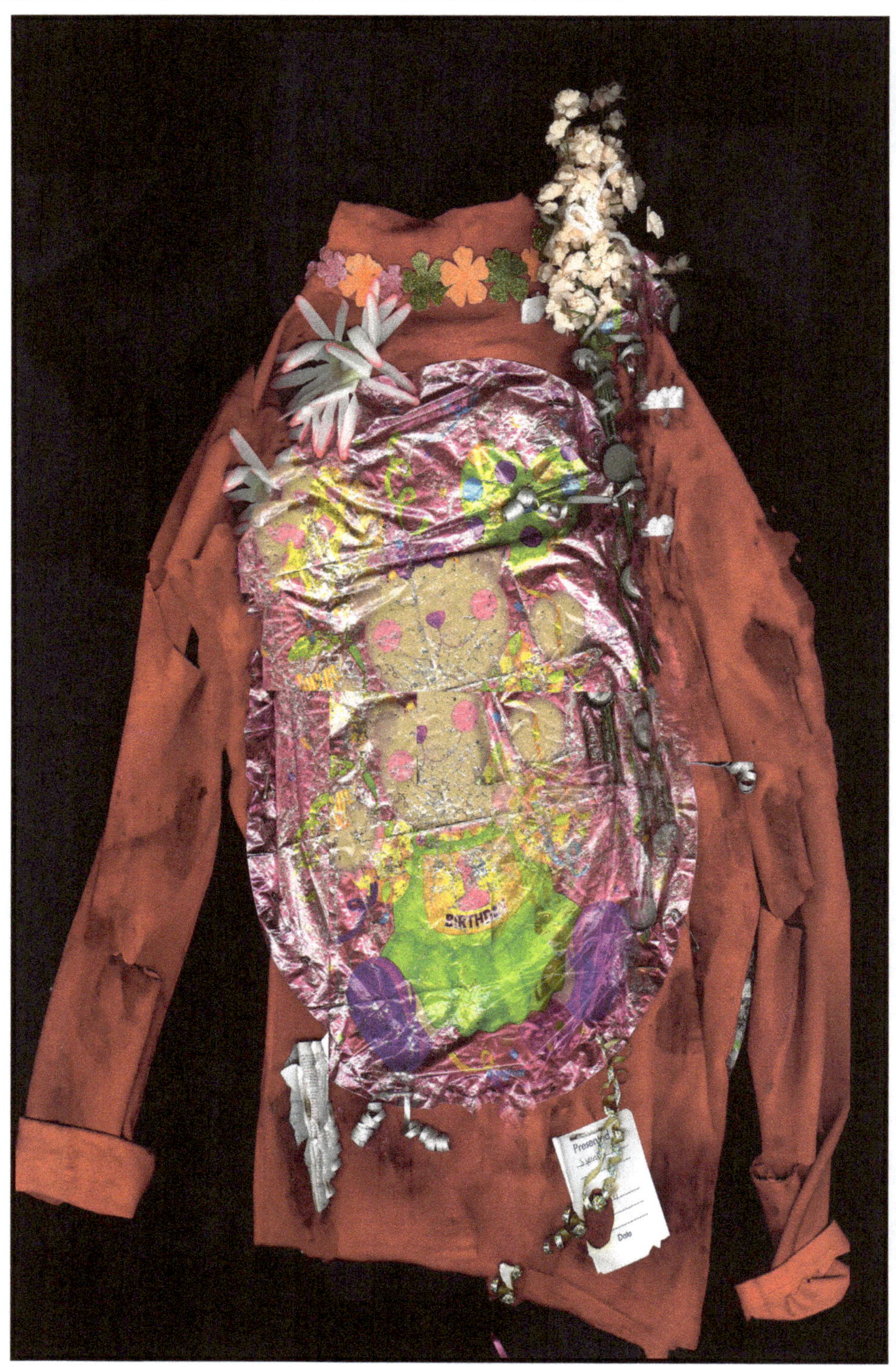

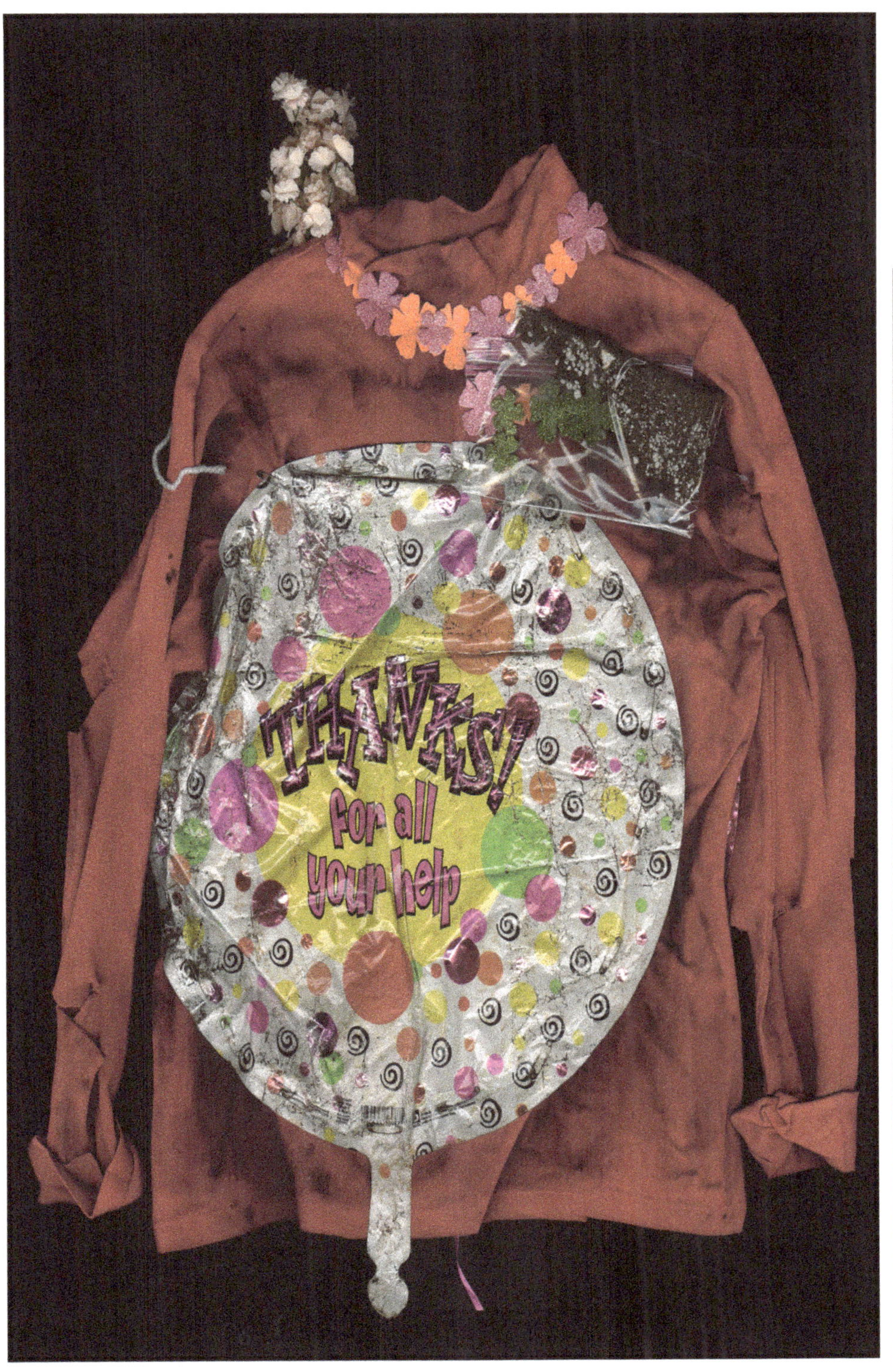

THANKS!
for all
your help

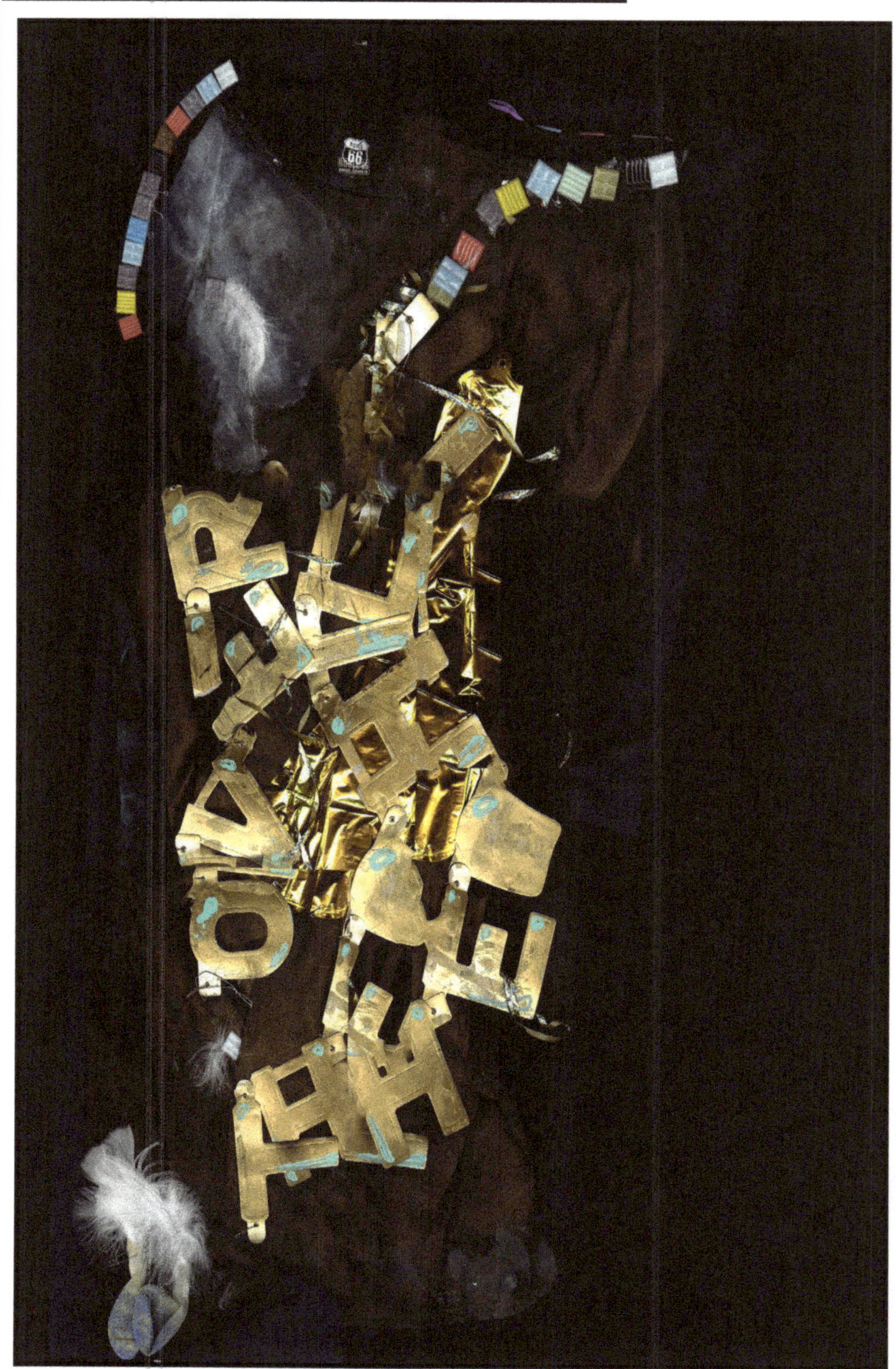

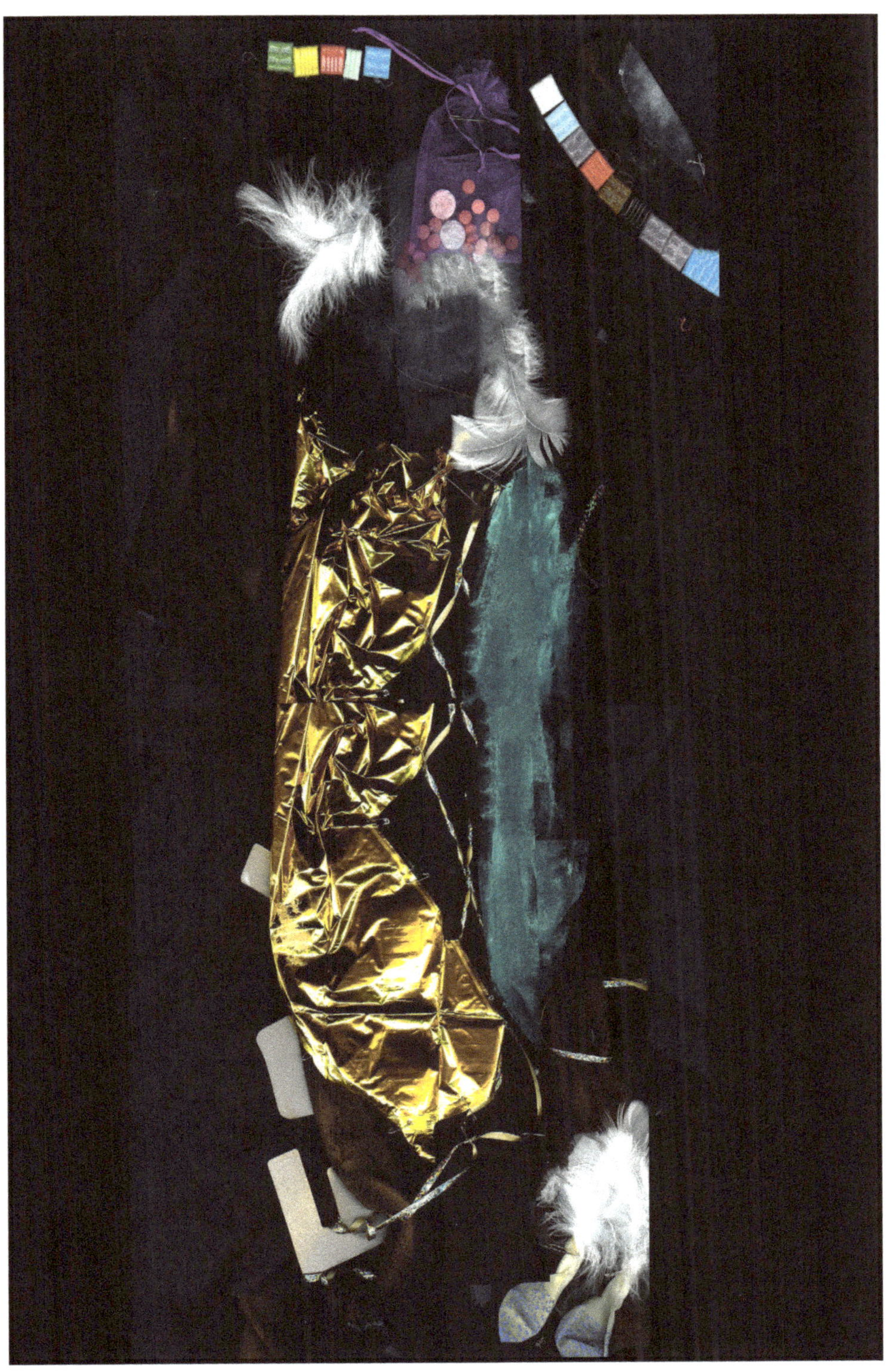

Self-portrait with Onion

April Rubasch

Cutting onions in the ruinous wood of butcher block
belonging once to my mother, I think of how she used to have horses,
ride them at dusk, and brush them with a hard-bristled hand brush.
Lazy acres filled with juniper and coated in dry Arizona sun
made her able in body and easy in heart.
She was kind in a way that makes people either cry or cringe,
candidly outspoken, yet easily dissuaded by the slopes of potential or change.
Children and a long marriage took her cheeks away,
left her hollow and veiny, the tiny blood vessels breaking under
the weight of her stories.
But most peculiar were the spells of outrage
when I no longer needed her kindness, denied her the pleasure
of her sacrifice, to which she had spent a lifetime bending and yielding
in twisted shapes until she had taken the form she would be.
It burns my eyelids like a smoky campfire, standing this close to her.
Are these tears forming on my hands my own?

Brother

Emily Rosier

Brotherhood crumbles as evil men hurt by passing on the street
possibility evaporates and smoke fills your lungs
whilst legs weaken as starving stomachs scream for something else but food
the clouds won't even rain, when begged to
the cruel sun beats though your lonely window
and you cry out for snow, and something you can weep for.

You failed the test this time, now everything is lost, without the key to unlock
the drawer with all your secrets, which might make them find you.
The pavement outside is full of last night's drinking,
the park is filled with people who have lost their love letters,
your home is full of ghosts.
you could empty your handbag and find a photo
but your bag is full of dirt and sand
from trips you never took and places you've forgotten.

Electricityscape

Min Ji Park

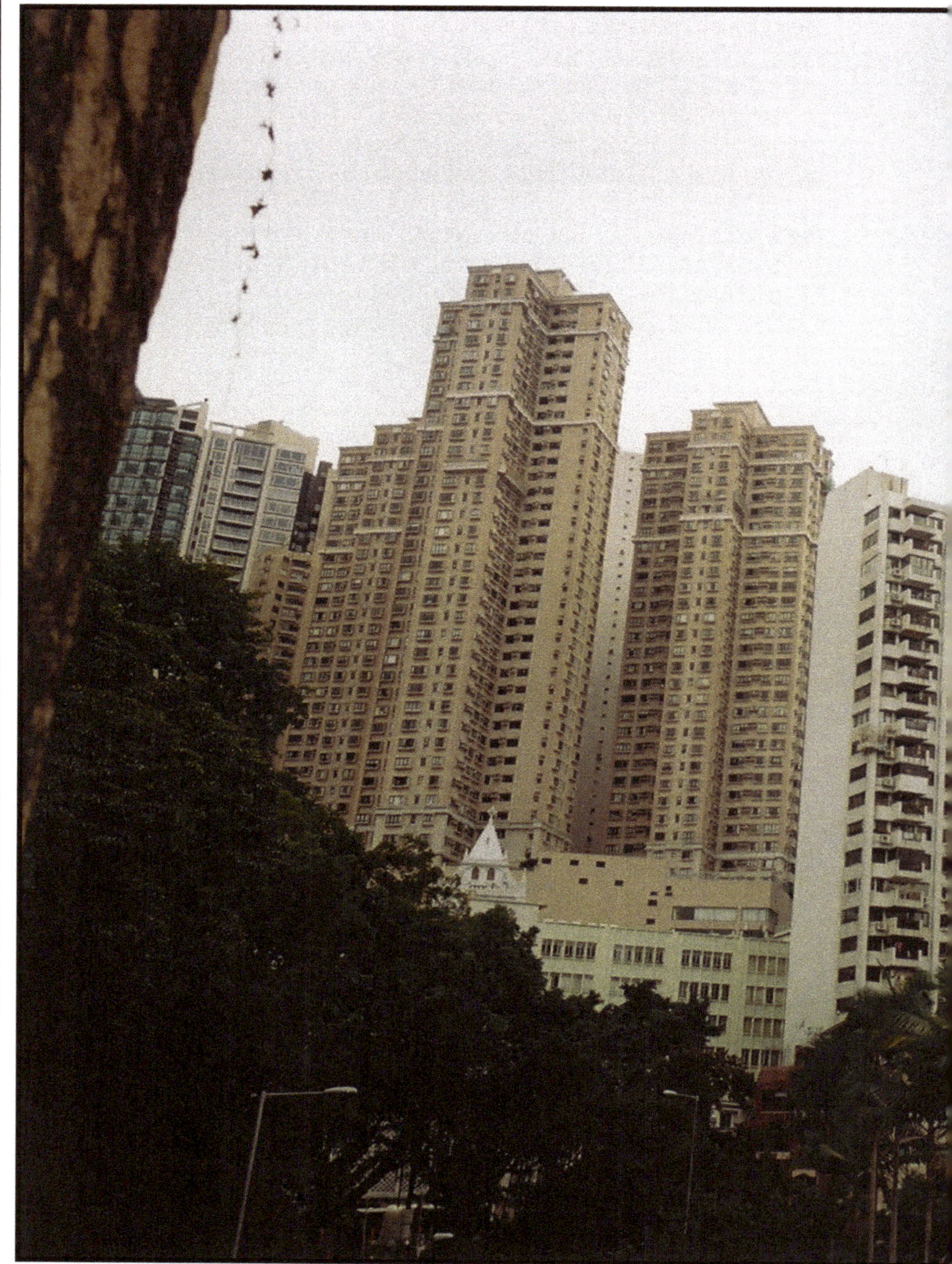

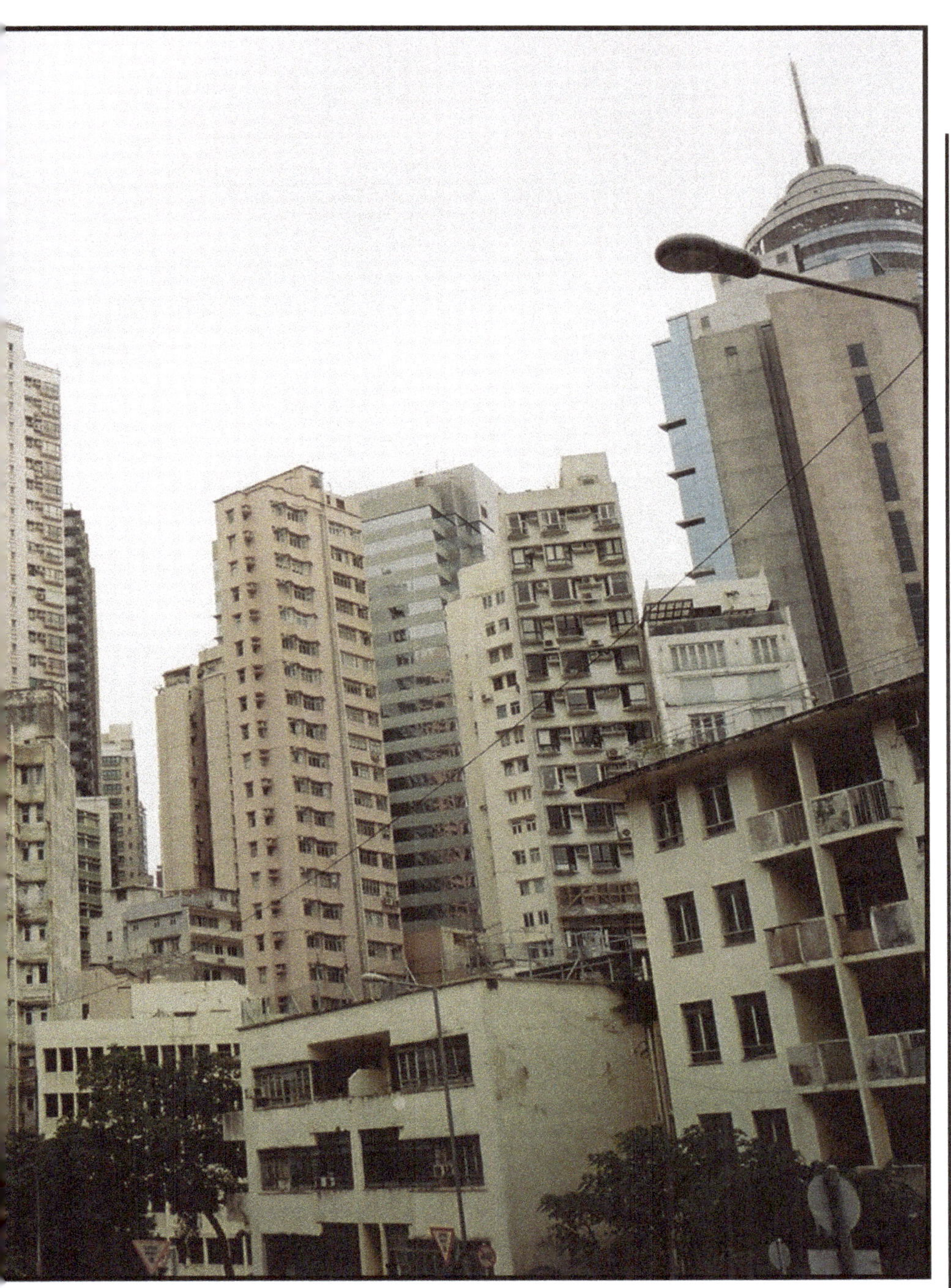

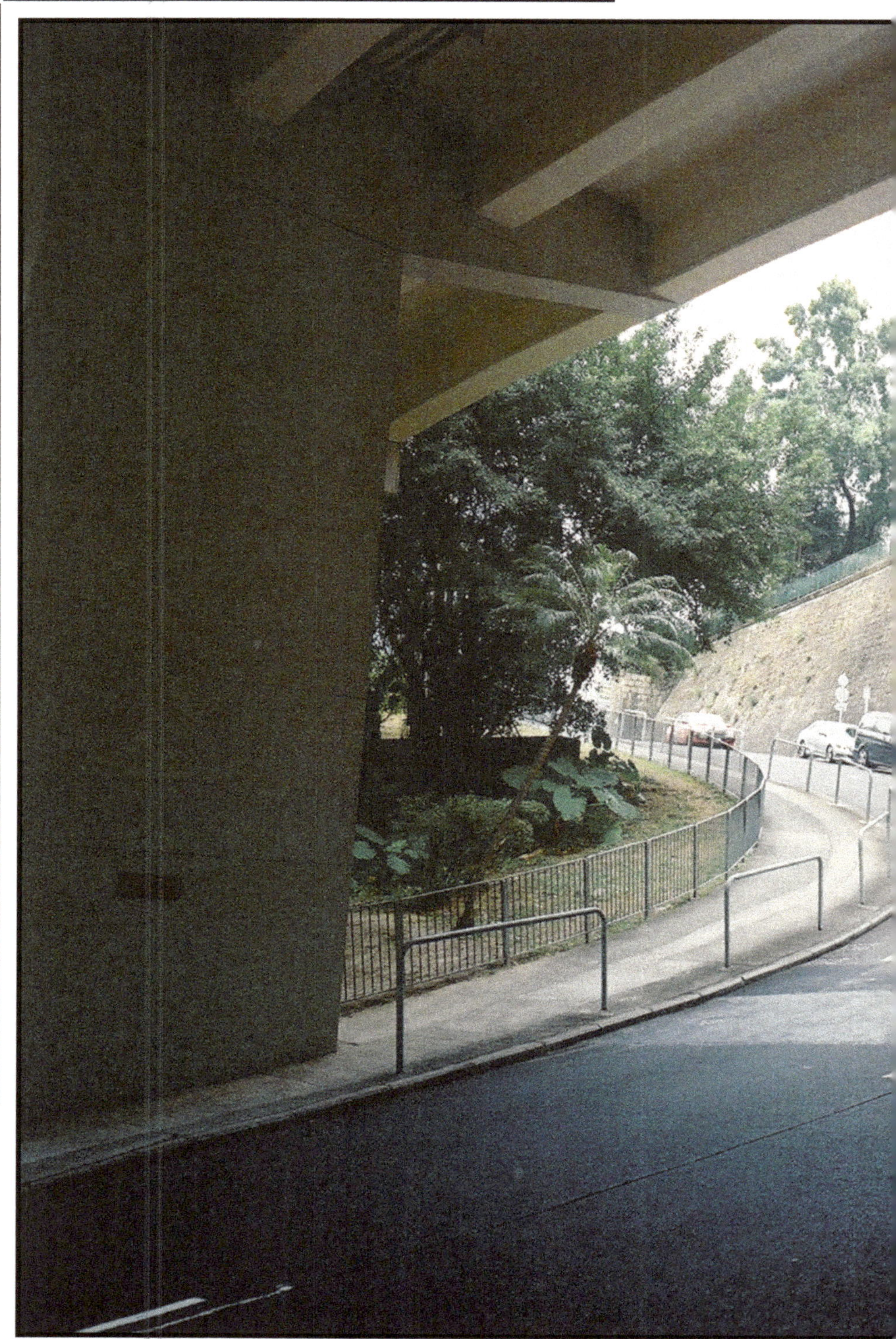

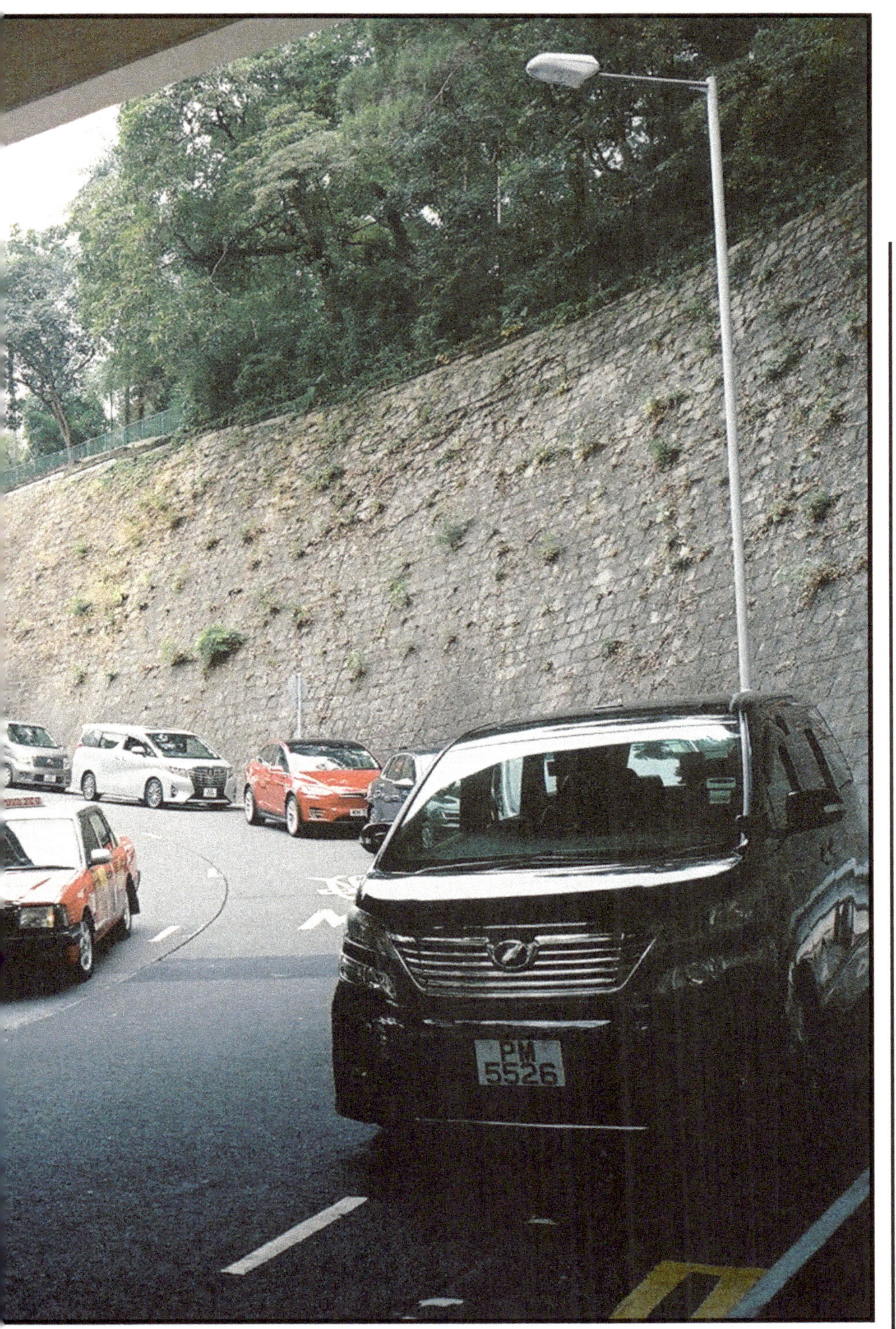

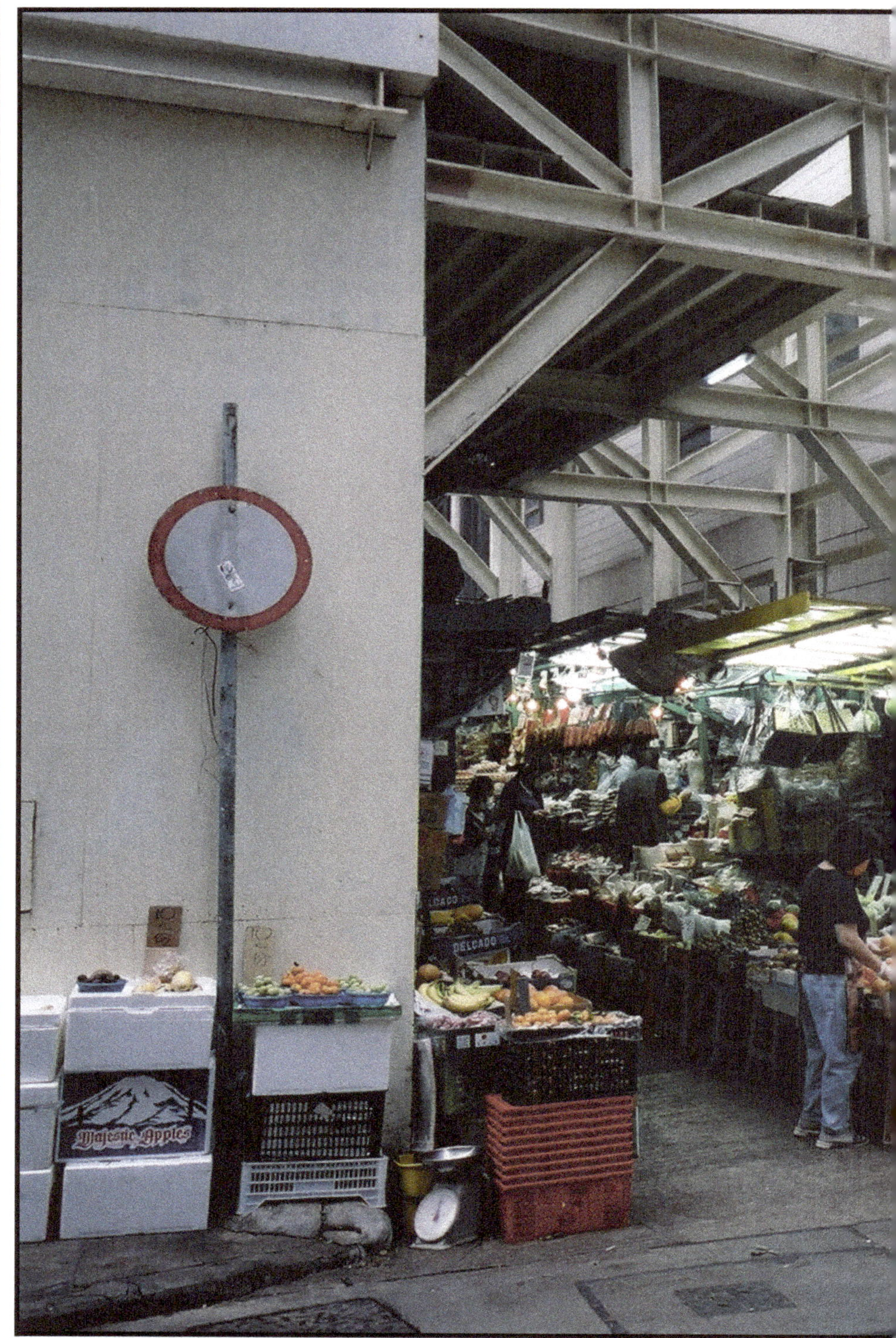

Majestic Apples

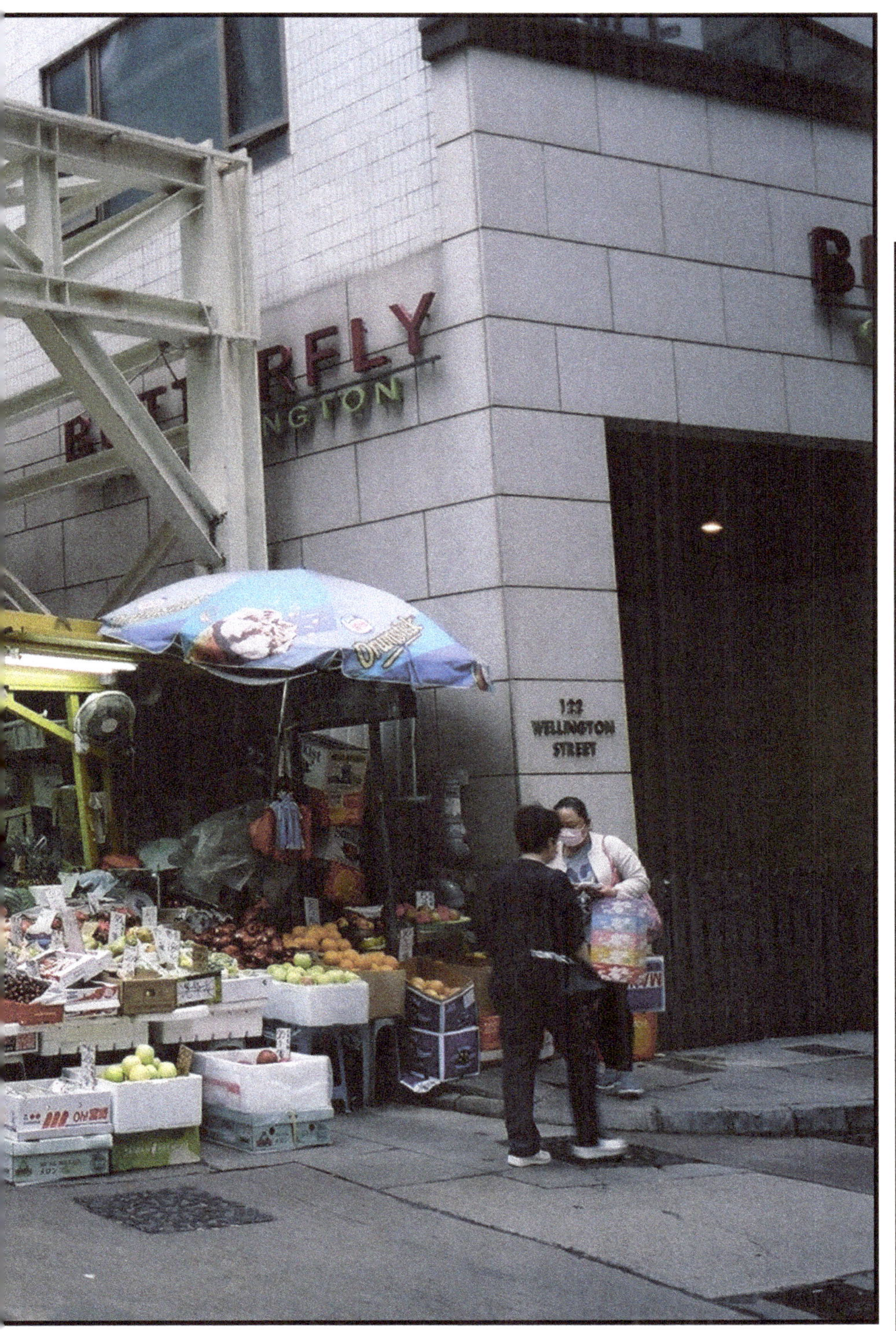
RFLY
NGTON
B
122
WELLINGTON
STREET

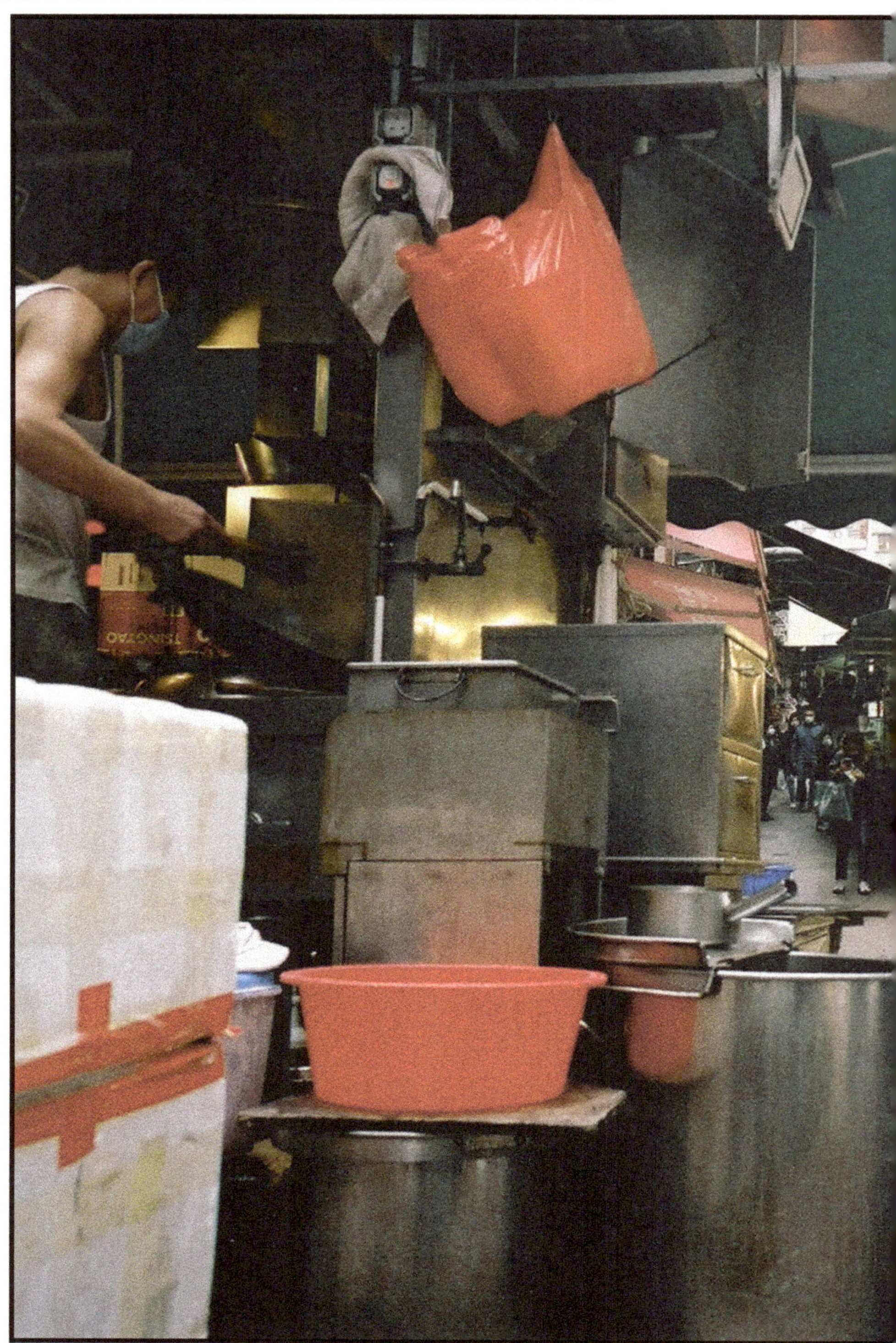

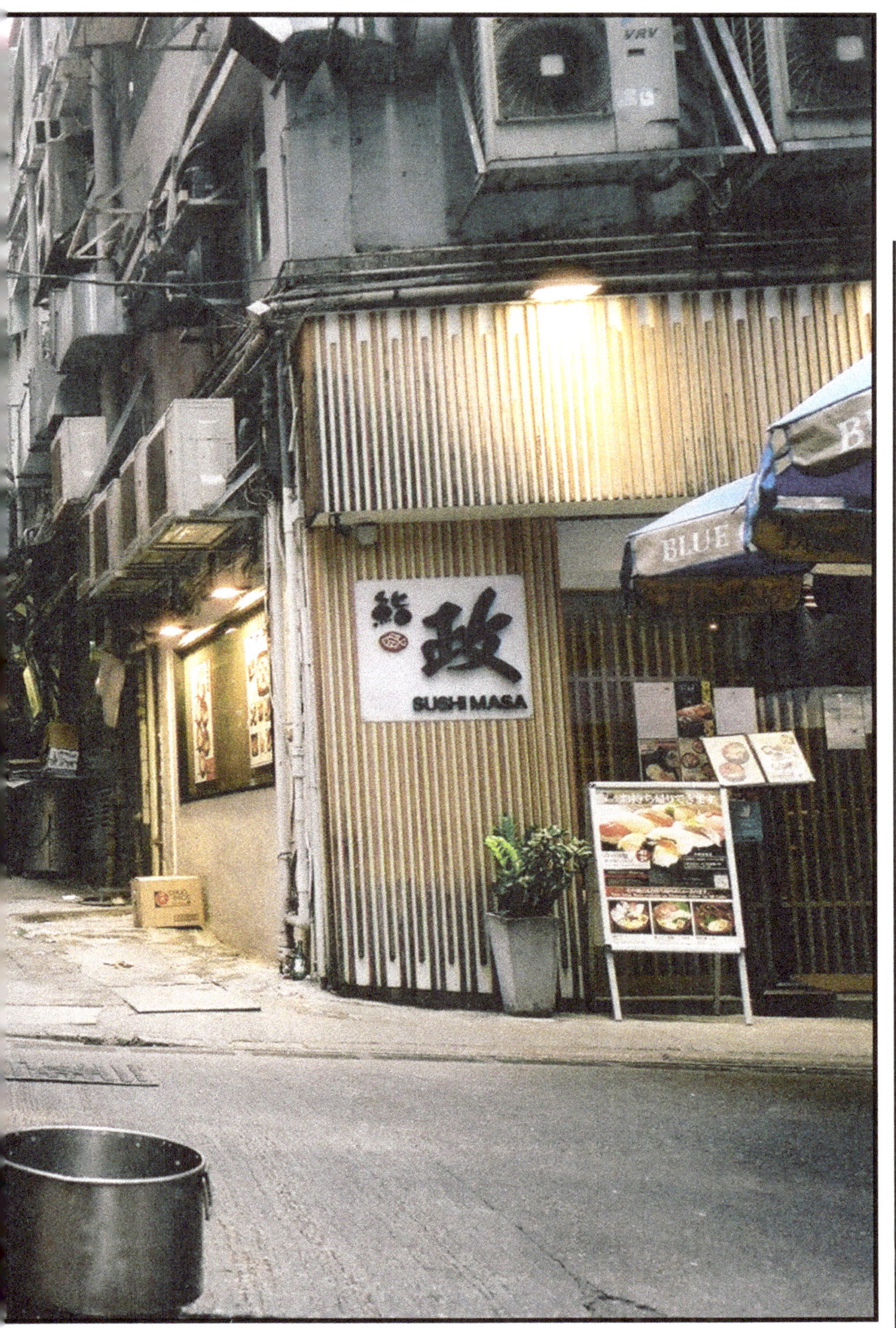

鮨
政
SUSHI MASA
BLUE

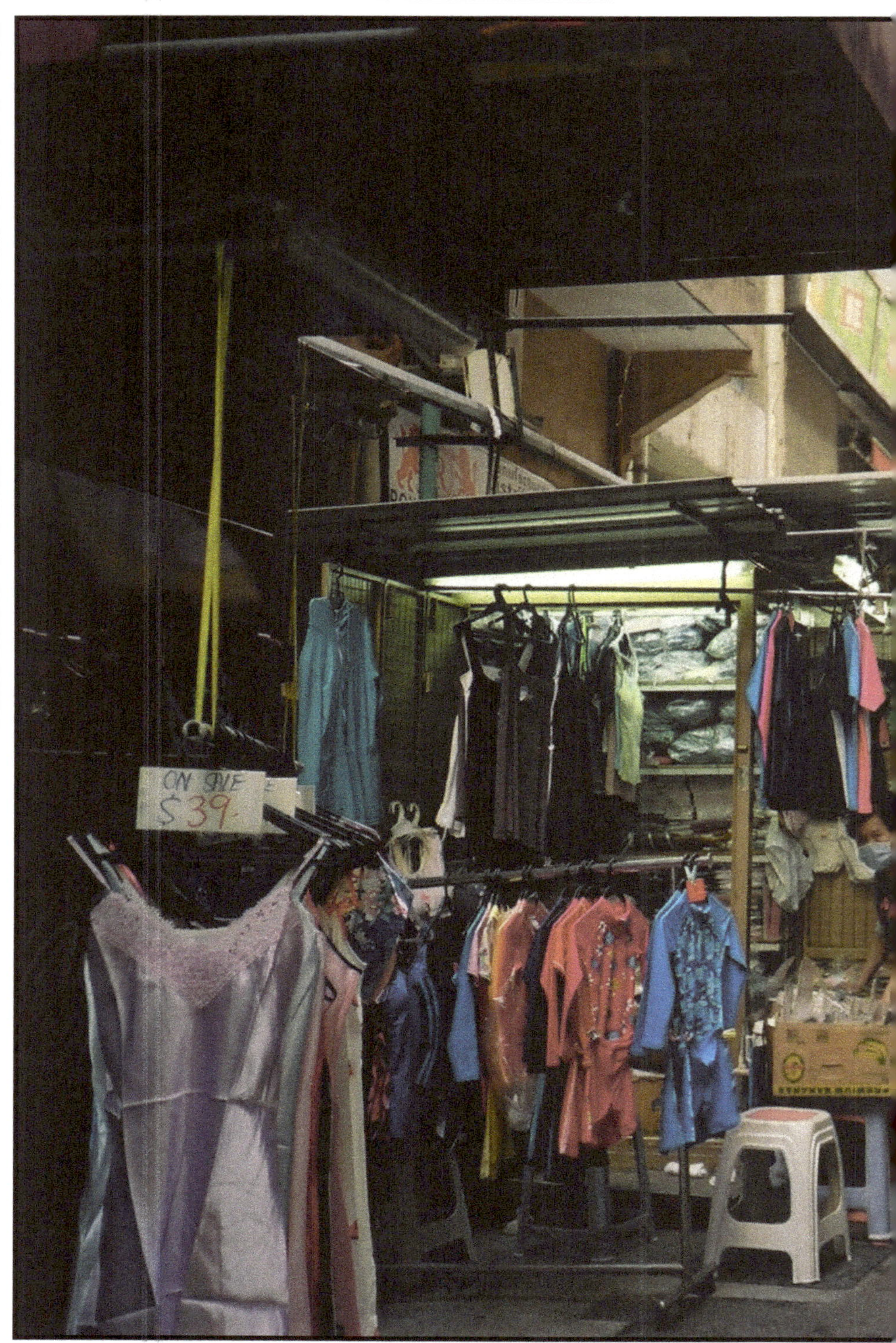

ON SALE
$39.

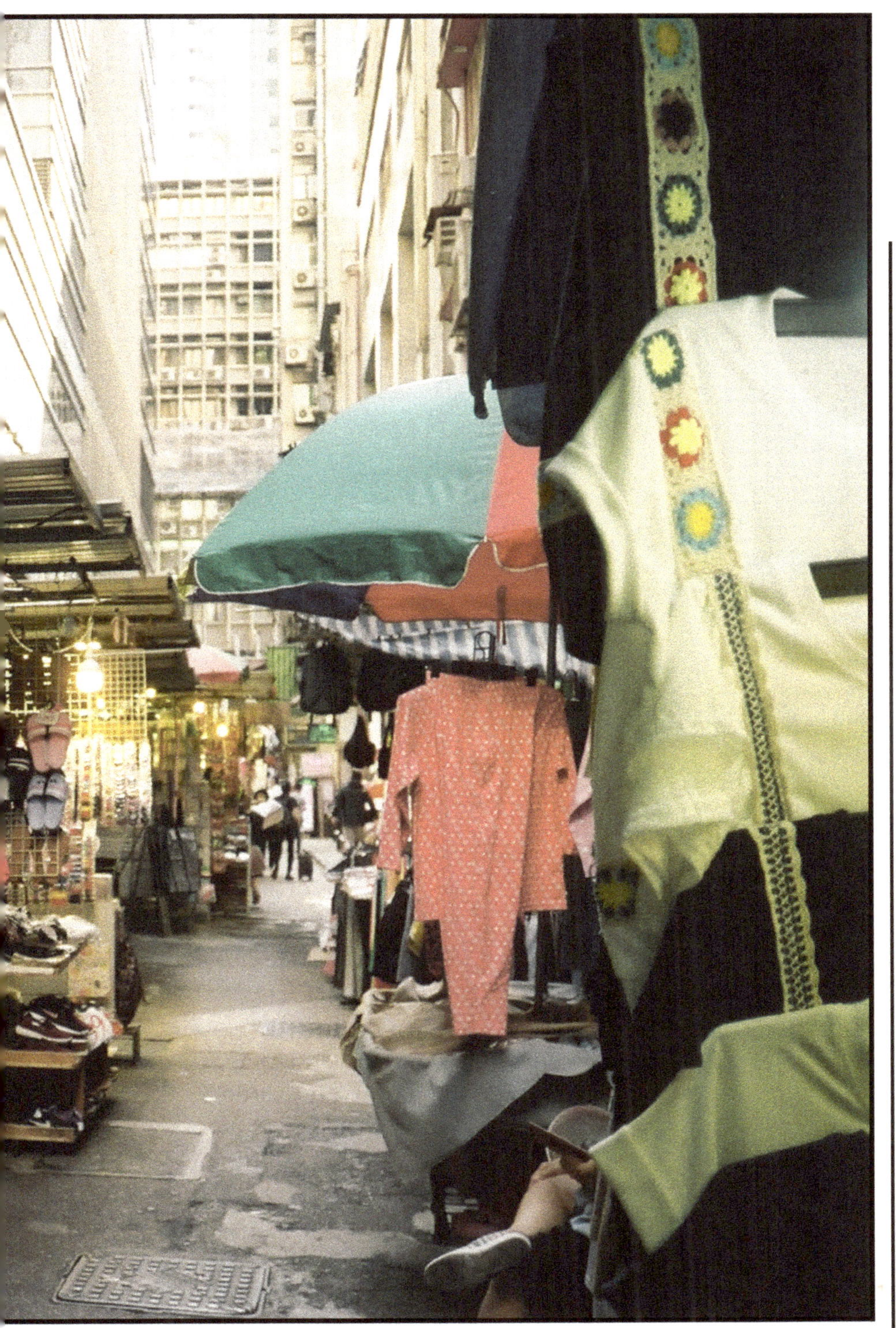

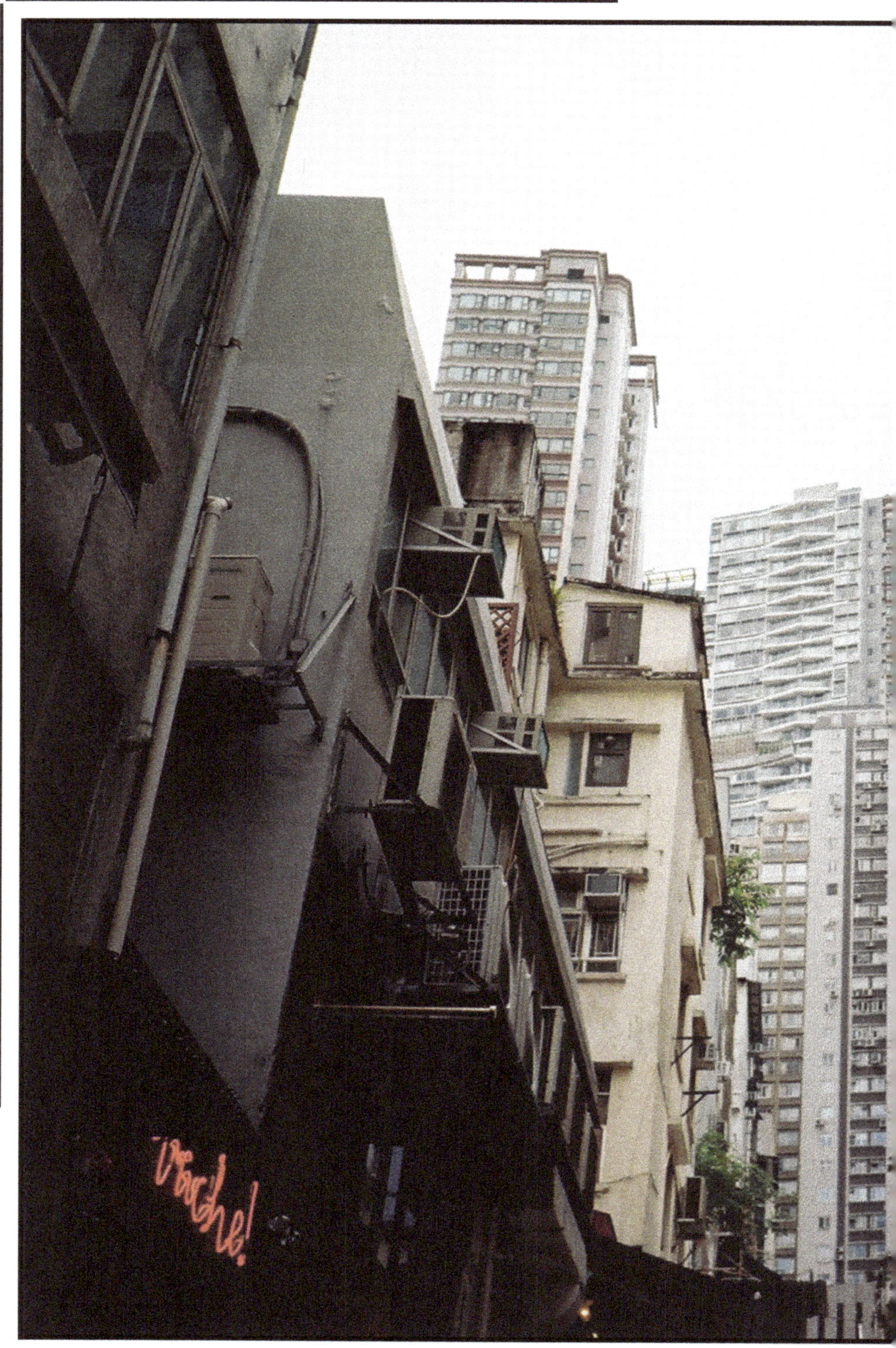

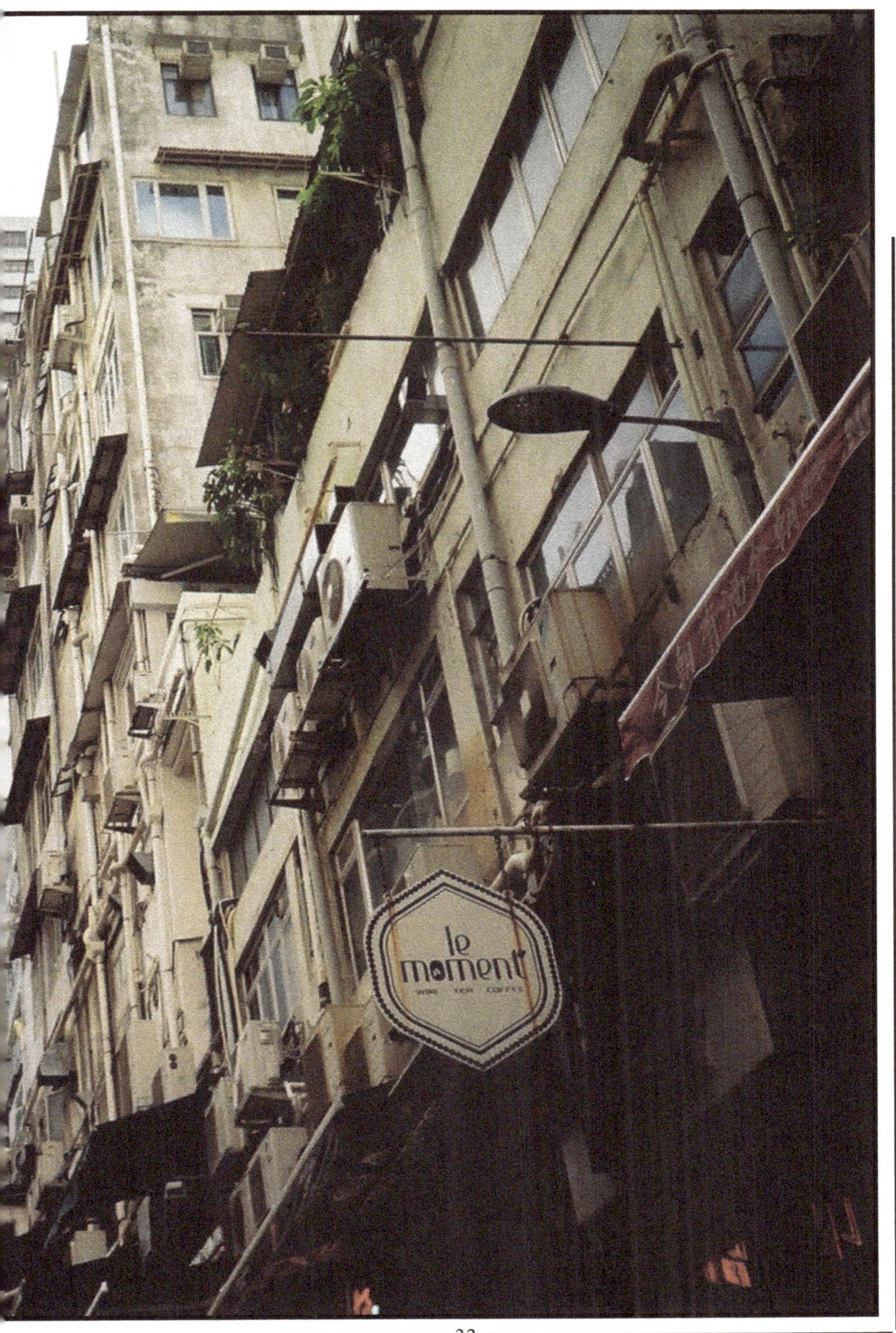
le
moment
WINE TEA COFFEE

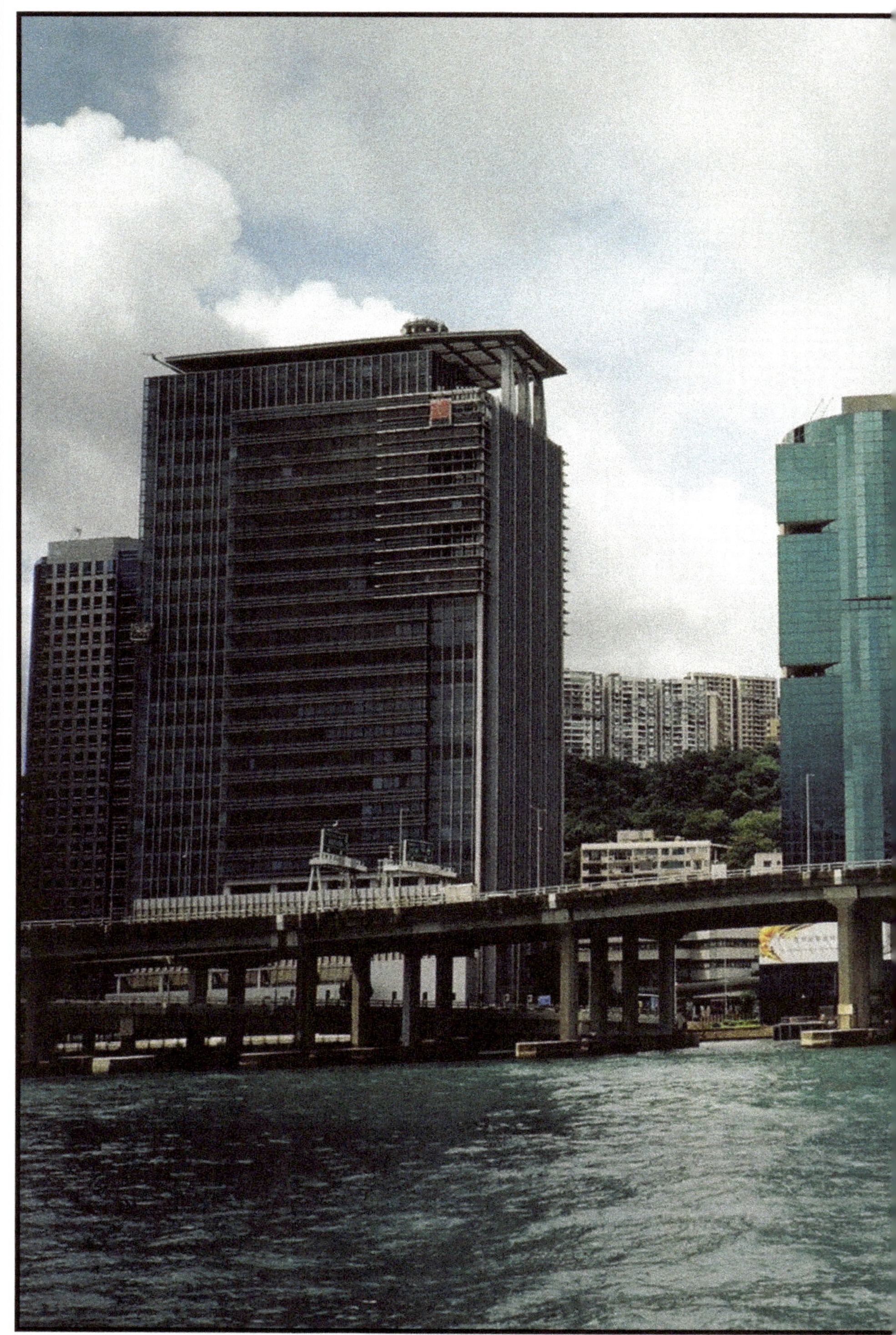

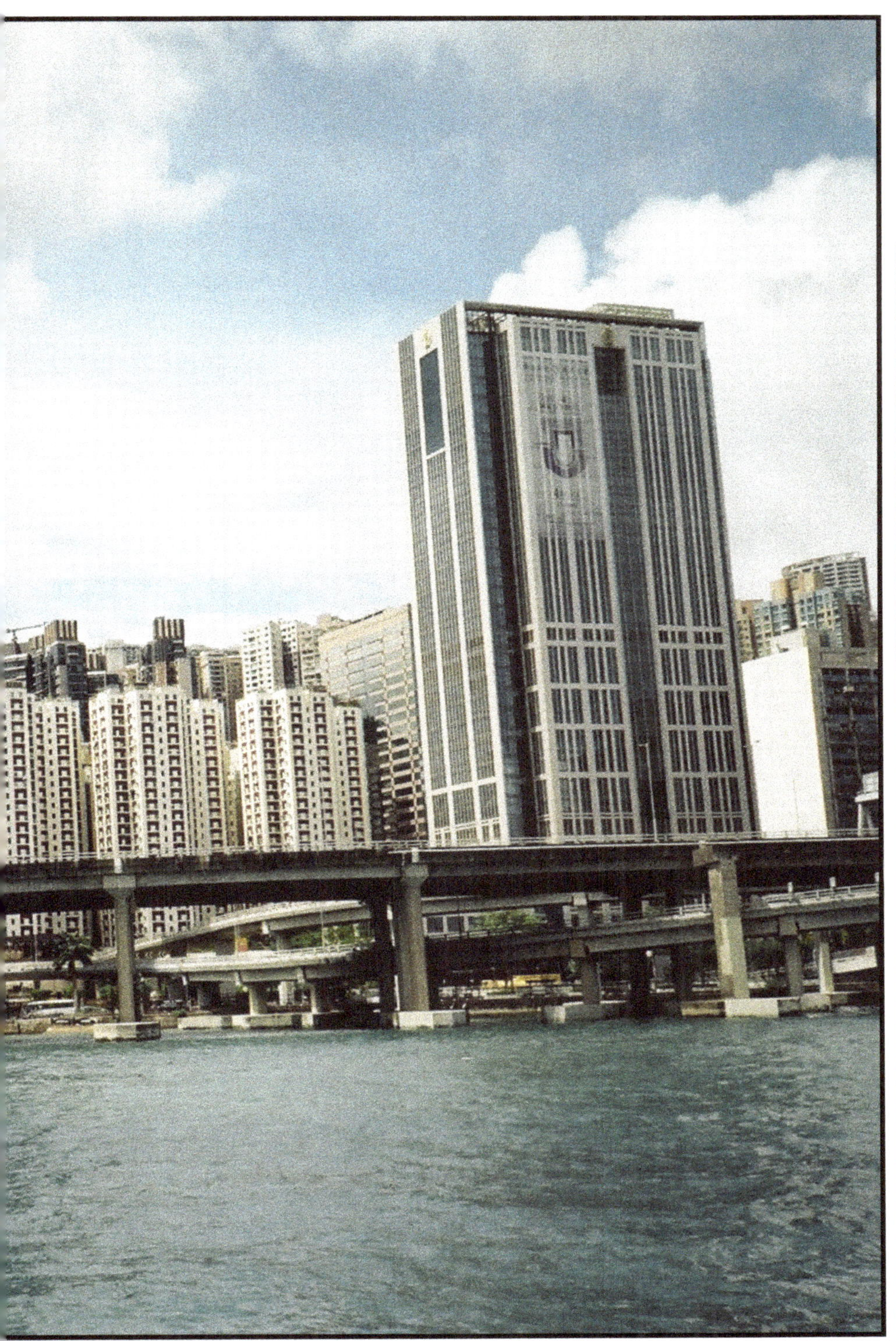

Floodplain

Corinne Hughes

If there's a rock at the edge of the world,
just tell me when,
tell me with red sand spilling out of your mouth,
with broken glass, with the same
rolling eyes like a lame mare,
a twisted turn of fate, the beating of a heart
in a cage, a leaf turned.

If to confess of time,
I have to speak in rivers with a face
lined with canyons, eyes sunken,
with a hand that grasps on nothing.
I toil a bit, lie back into something soft,
but I am only waiting
for you to tell me when.

Tell me with a million pieces of cloth and thread,
build me a dress to sway in as I fall,
embroider the visions of flowers, cascading rivers,
trees thick and tall, but let everything fit into my palm.

I miss people, their shaking hands,
glares slicing the air.
I miss their shoulders in shrugs,
the weeping, the dances. I want to be
beside them, brushing out the knots in
their hair with blades of
wheat and blue stem. I want to beg of me,
of everything solid afoot, winding down,
in a glow.

If you do not tell me when, then tell me where,
tell me why and tell me every time.
I will try to understand,
tell me with broken nails,
I will try to,
tell me with stuttering lips,
no need for meaning,
and nothing I ever needed to know.

Hypatia

Jose Varghese

Rusty specks rise from dried up blood on
the steps of the bibliothèque, to be claimed
by the amber-gray sun that'd kept her rising
intellect on an endless ellipse, stuck forever

to the painful orbit of ritualistic instruction.
The clouds extend their icy arms to take her
elements to preserve them in their bosoms
till they melt in grief, to pour down torrential

rains to the seas, Aegean or Arabian, over the
musical movement of mermaids navigating
mysterious circuits beyond humans, or to the
lands, over the geometrical dance moves of

girls whose eyes sparkle with light sprouting
from her disseminated spirit, and yes, Helios.

Breakdown

Cree Cullars

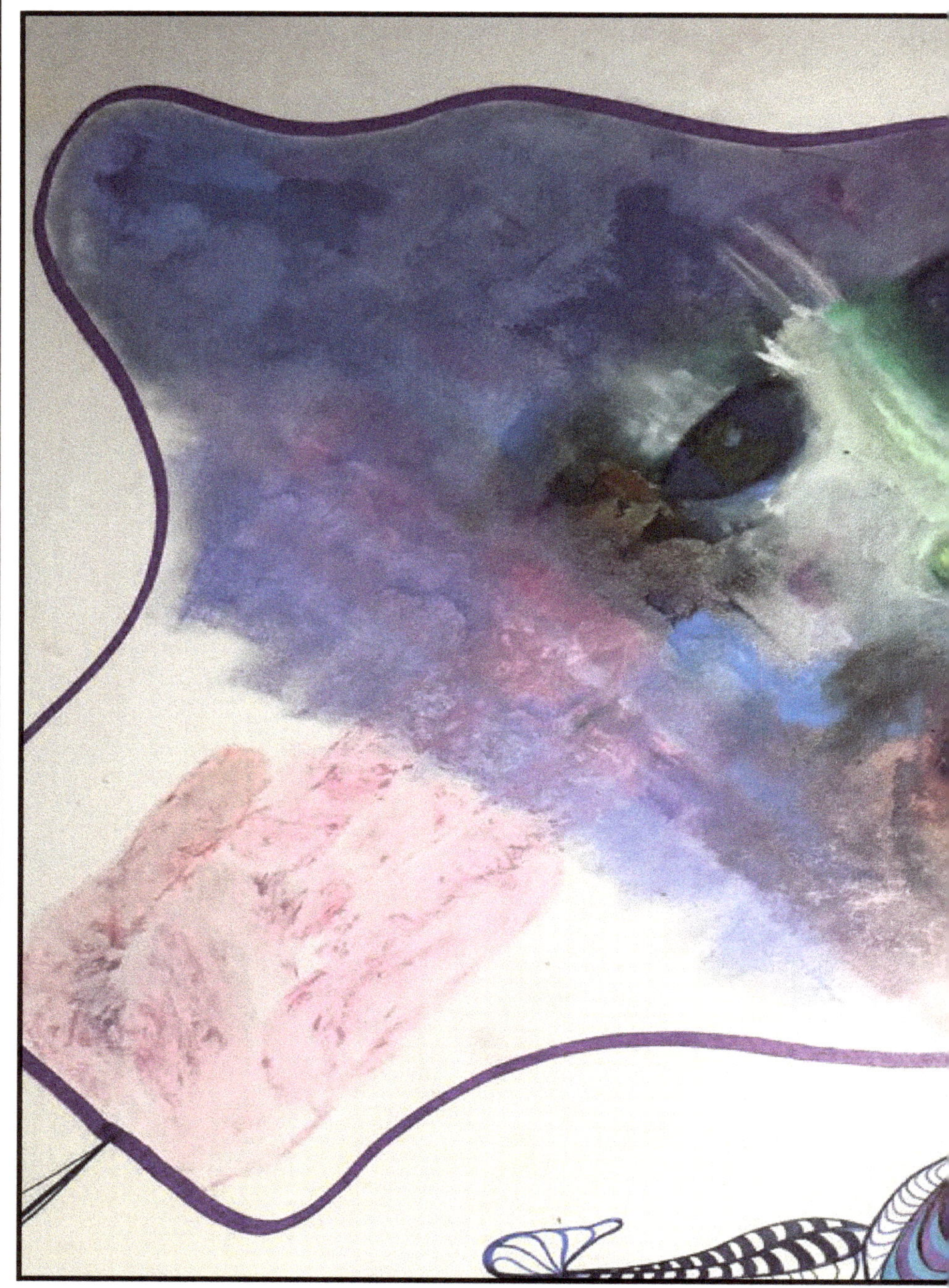

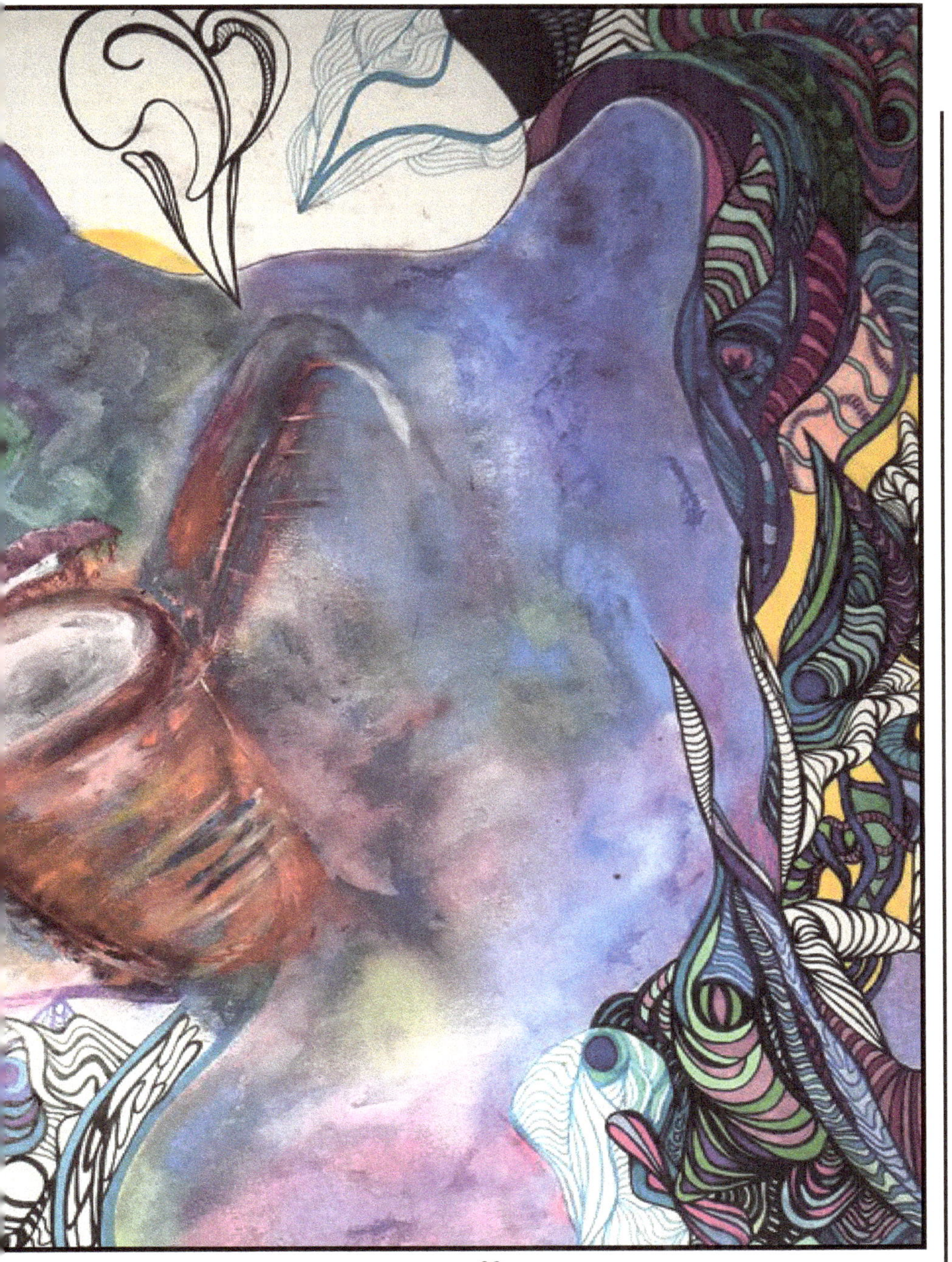

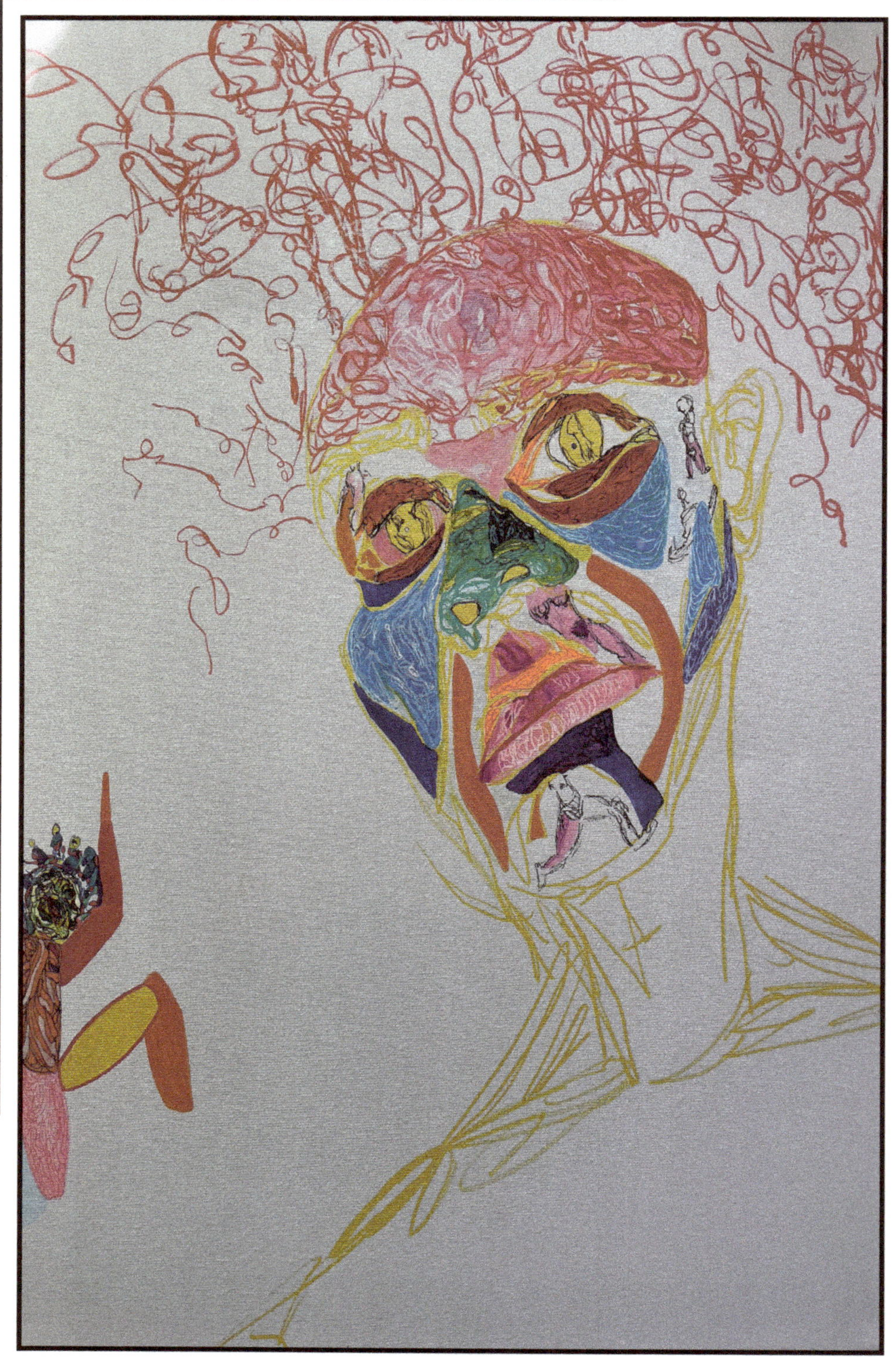

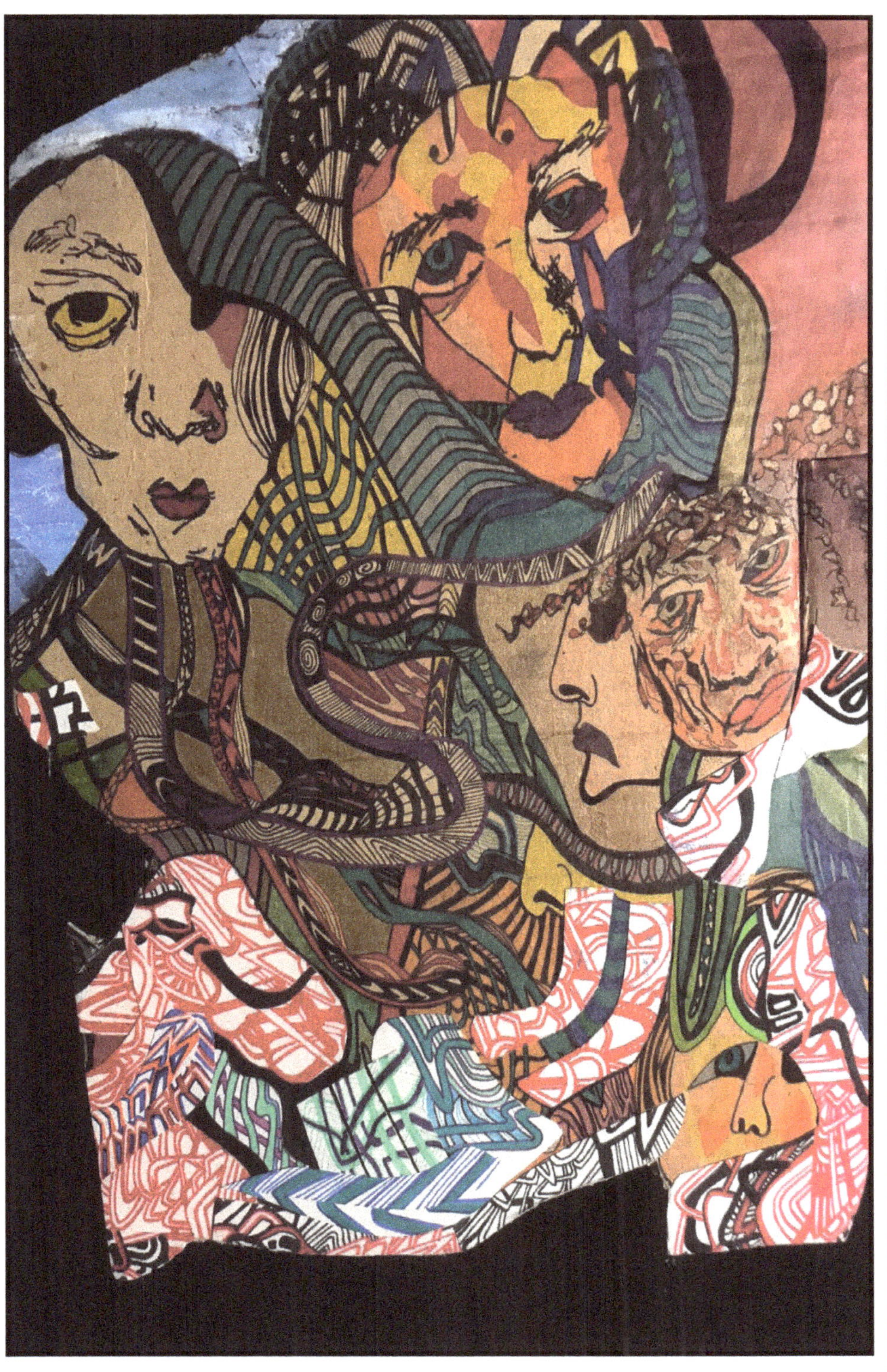

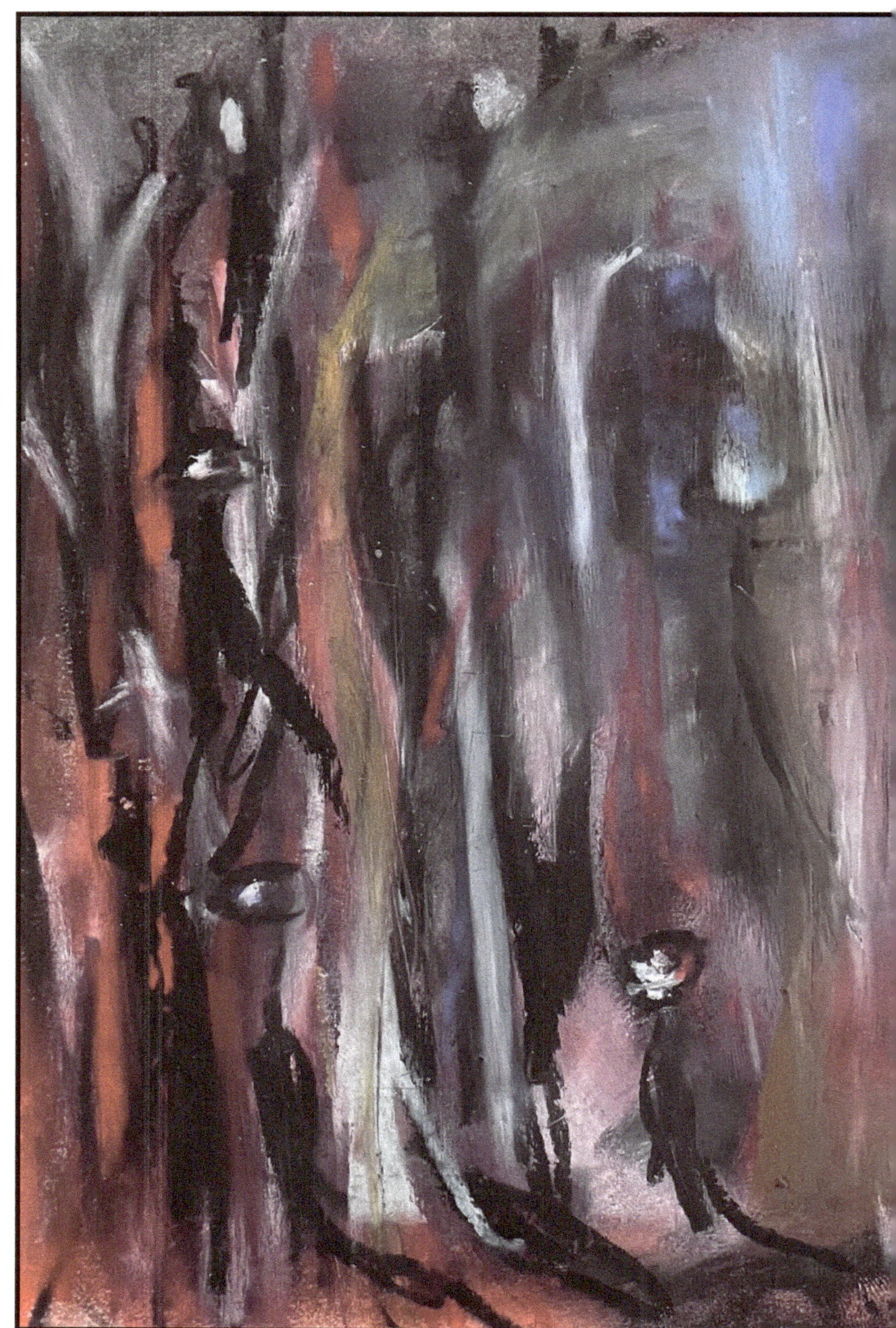

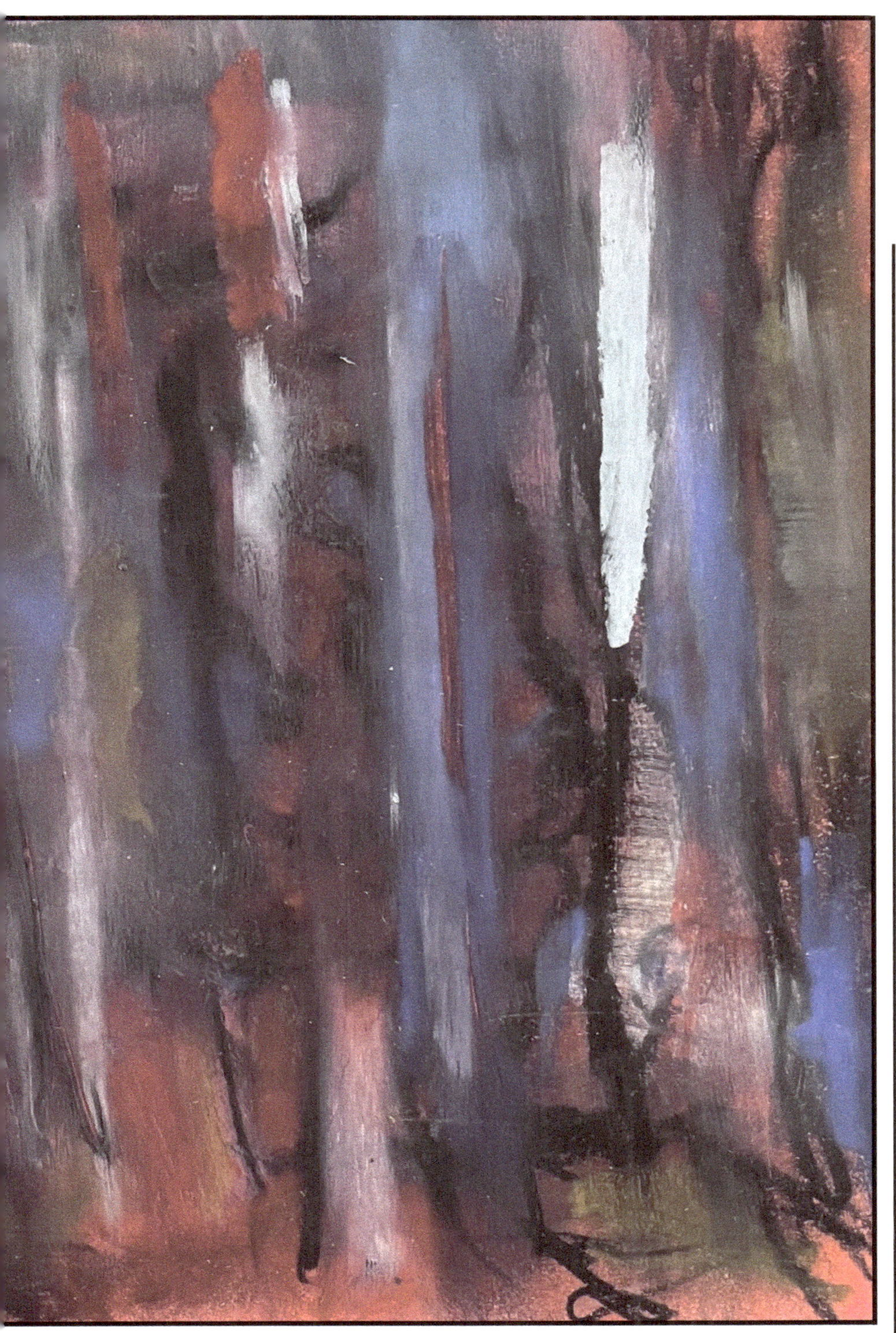

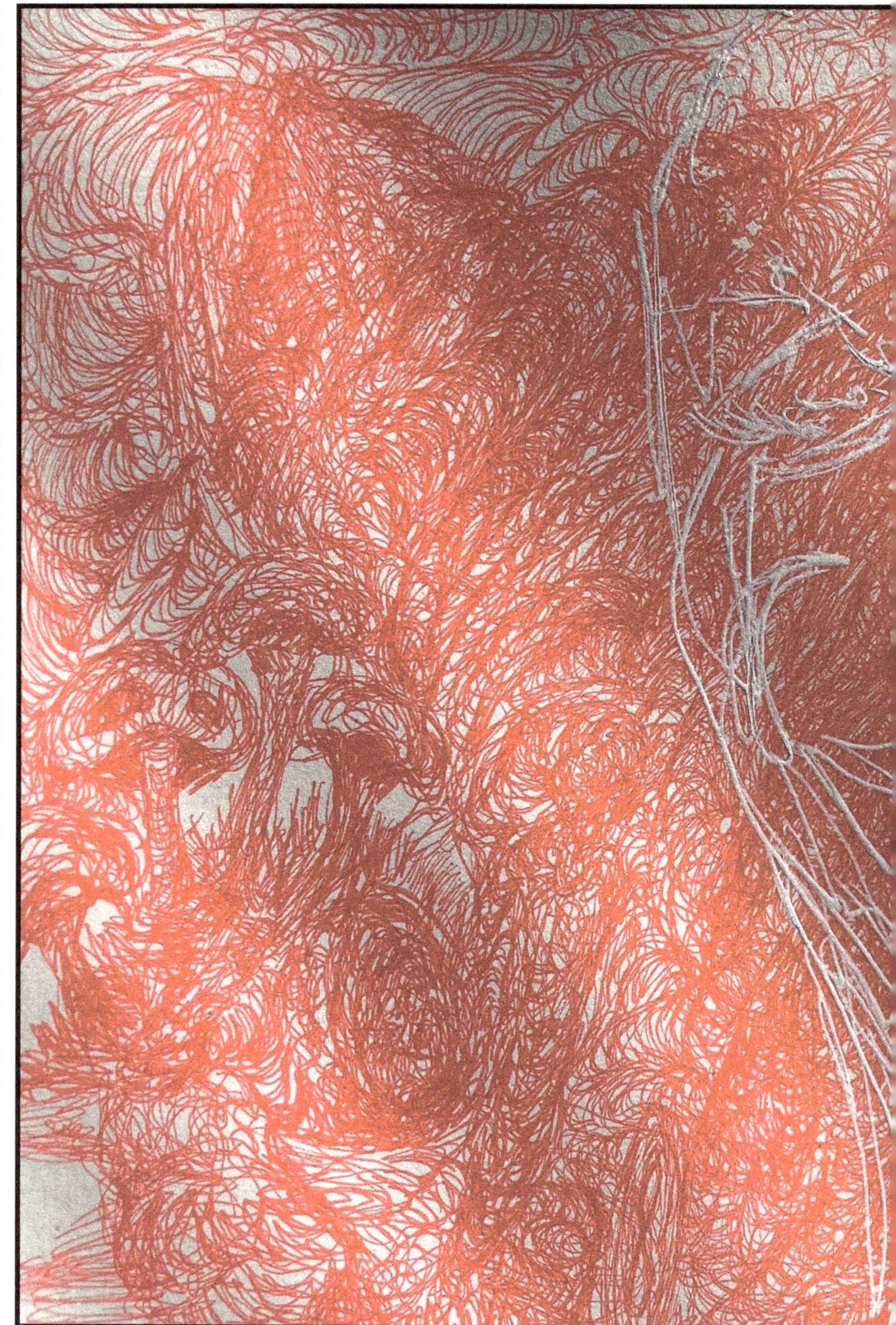

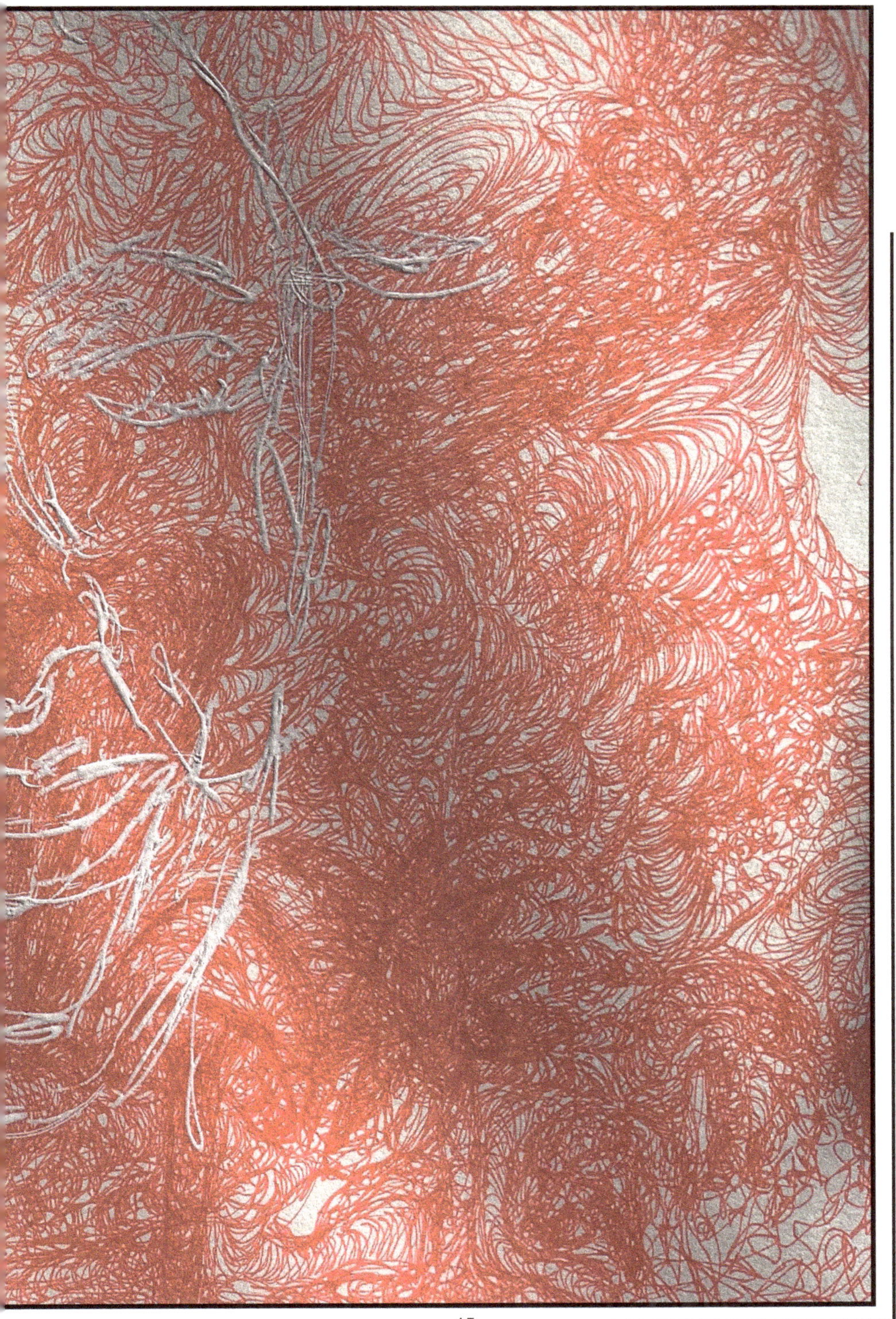

Losing Them...

Jodie West

If only I had gathered you
into a pile of firm remembrances,
stones to mark the favored
plots from childhood

before they scattered like rocks
on the bottom of a riverbed,
abrasion settling the jagged
edges into dull, rounded forms,

memories blurred with the smoothing
time has wrought.

Such memories crush themselves
into a cusp of fondness, dulled stones
rushed over the cliff of passing time

like a toy lost in the shuffling
from one parent's home to another's,
the swiftness carrying them to some
undesignated shore.

But I remember the laughter,
the giggles of children
as uninhibited as geese honking
at the extra crust of bread.

Names now belong
in that wordless chasm where time
flies to lose itself,
but the joy those giggles beckon
have become
the haven for all else I have forgotten.

Art Midlife

Mark Christopherson

So it took me years to be born
from that womb of cigarette smoke
and strobe lights, emerging half dazed
and late on arrival, the waiting room
empty and the coffee cold on the table.
They didn't leave in a hurry and who
could blame them. There are some
born so fast these days you have to lean back
or be slung with amniotic fluid, insolent
beautiful babies, others dropped into rice
fields with weather darkening the sky.
Of course a few are born premature
and wind up backing down the warm
canal, mouthing a slight apology to their
disappointed audiences. Me, I'm the latest
of all comers; born to words at last, born
to the melodies of weather, born to
the mournful ballad, finally born.
It wasn't so bad in there, really.
You can get chatter on the dial but
the reception is spotty, and there is a straight
pipe to the fastest food. The distractions
are of course relentless. But we are inevitably
out, and for me it's through this cancelled reception,
stepping over magazines and out into the parking
lot. Perhaps I'll write a line to coax
another middle-aged child into the full bloom
of the early silence. It's such a dark flower,
this new envelopment, such a fat hour to be born
into the incessant labors of art.

Loved Again.

Andrea Cueva

Pressed flower,
Sealed between clipped pages of wax,
In a yellow envelope, this genie's lamp,
Hidden away in a book on a shelf,
"Driving through Cuba"
Published -- 1988,
Thirty-five years after her immigration,
Now resting solely with me.
Red petals, like the flag's only triangle,
Peek between waxed pages of white,
I rub my fingers through the opening,
Whispering to the genie of her past,
Scrawled on the back, *Maria*
"Abuelita, quién es esta letra?"
I say to echoes of no one, then carefully
Pinch the thin, dark, dried stems.

I resign to the floor, dusty, musty,
With no care for the seat of my pants,
And I search for more flowers within this,
An outdated book of lost lands.

Road Trip, California to Idaho

Roger Camp

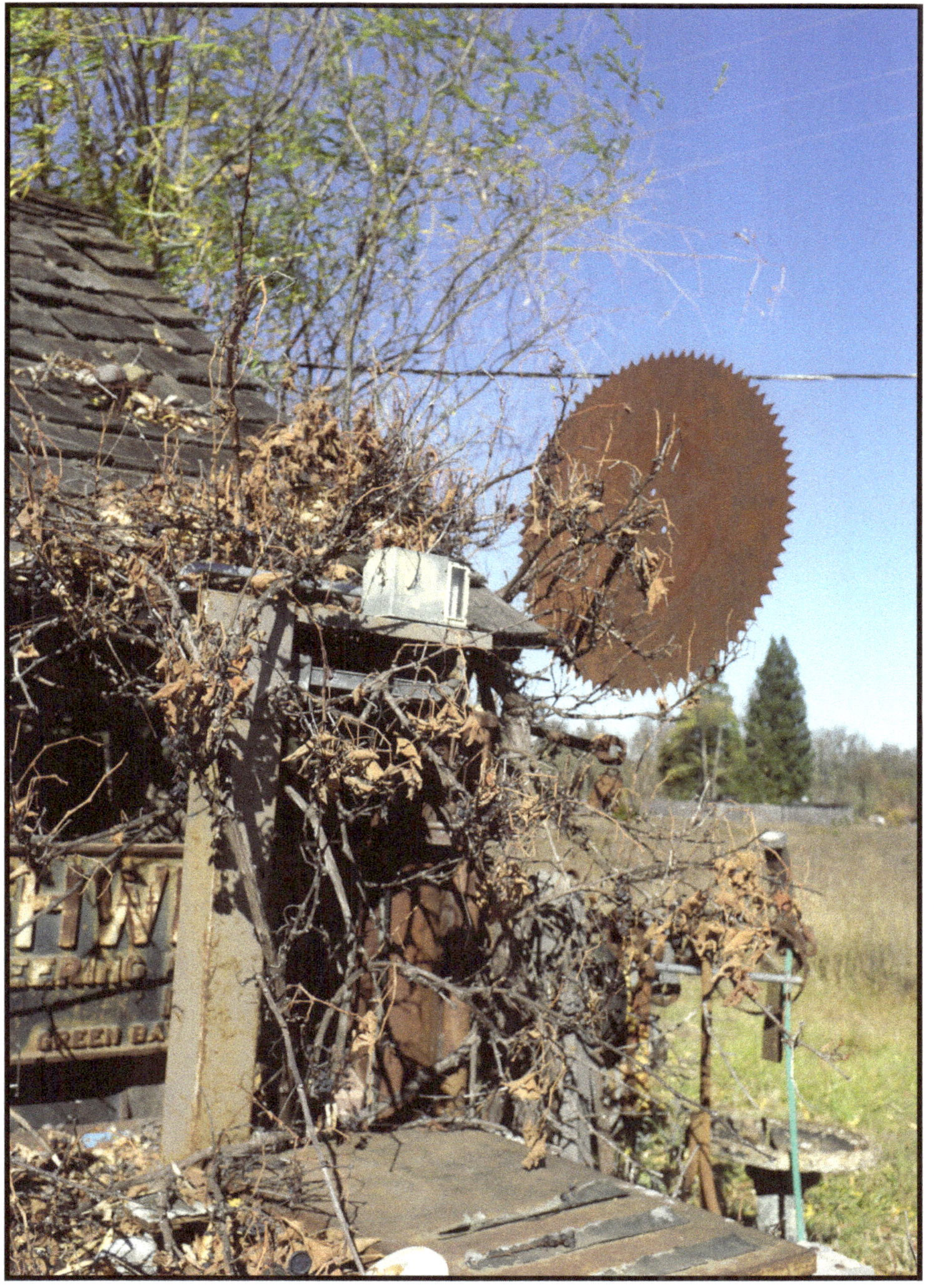

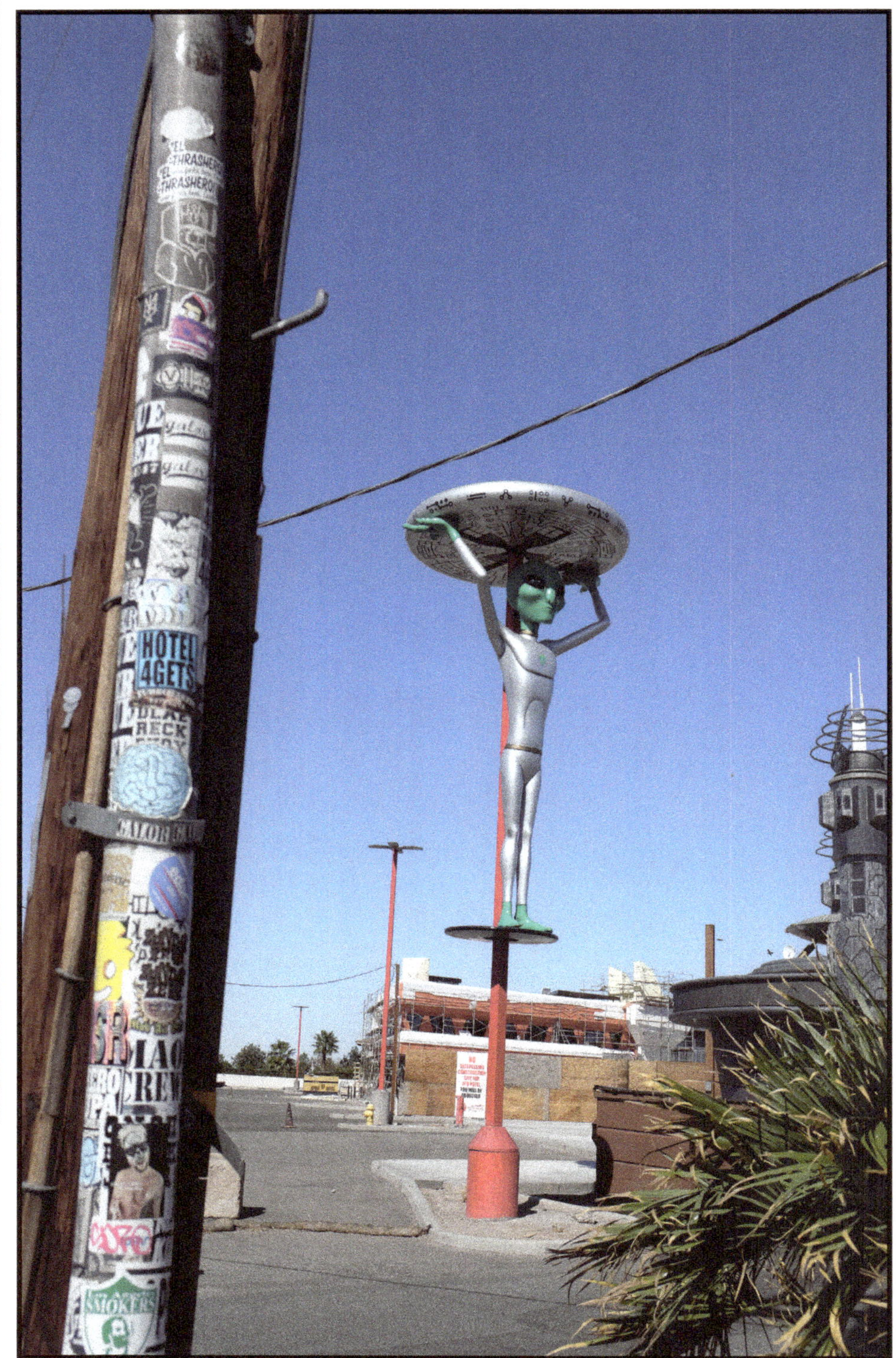

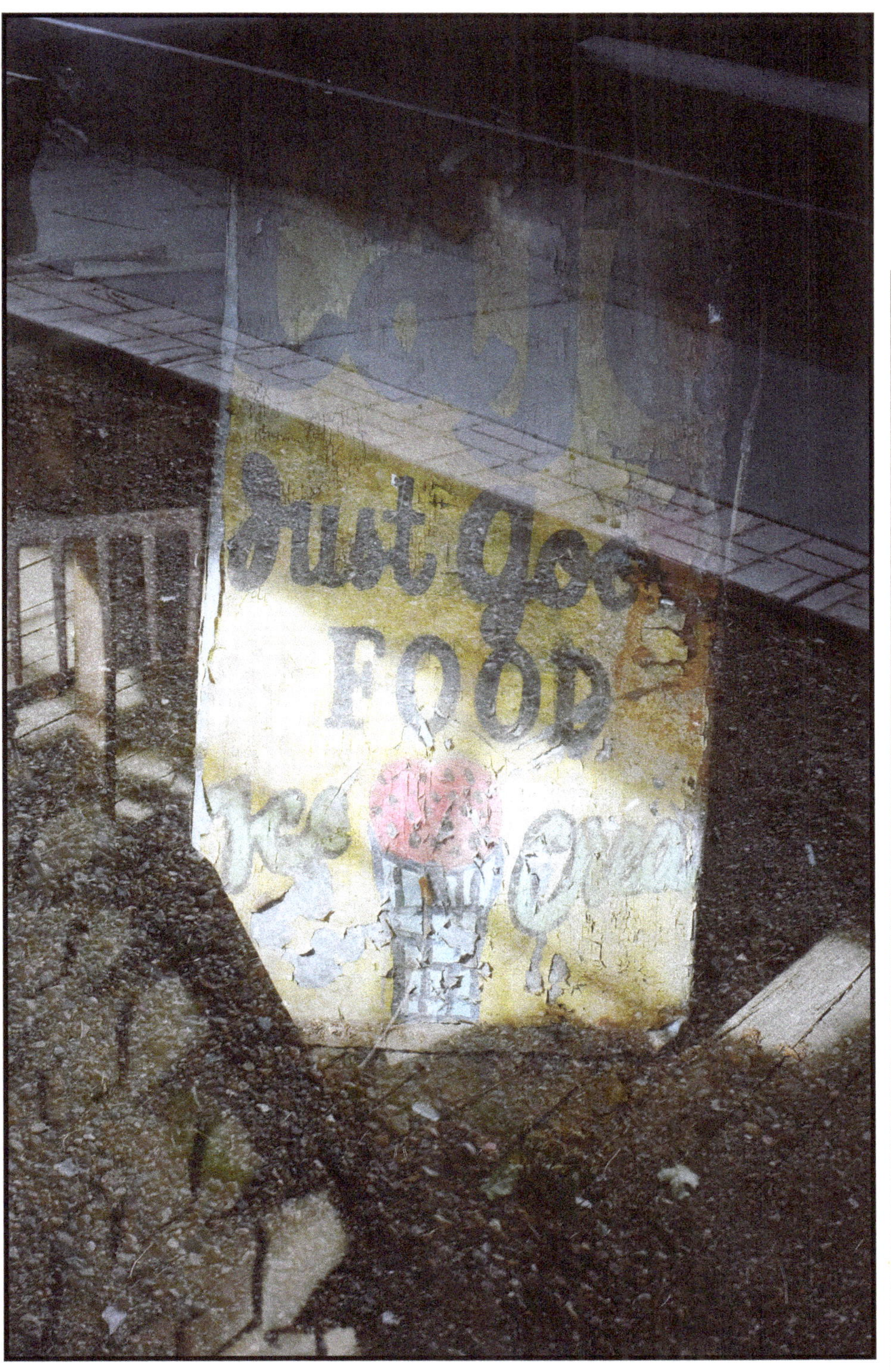
Just Good
FOOD
Ice   Cream

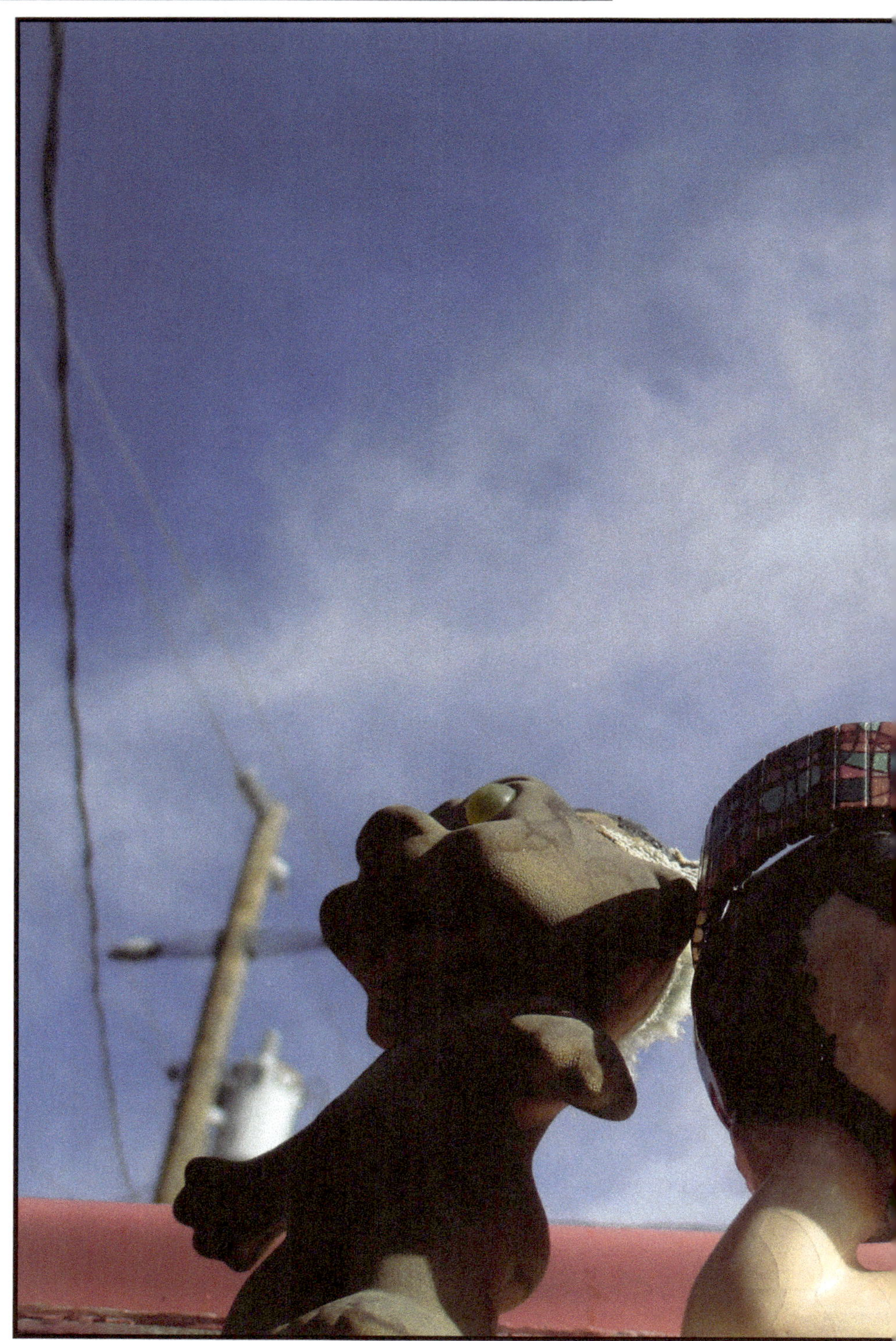

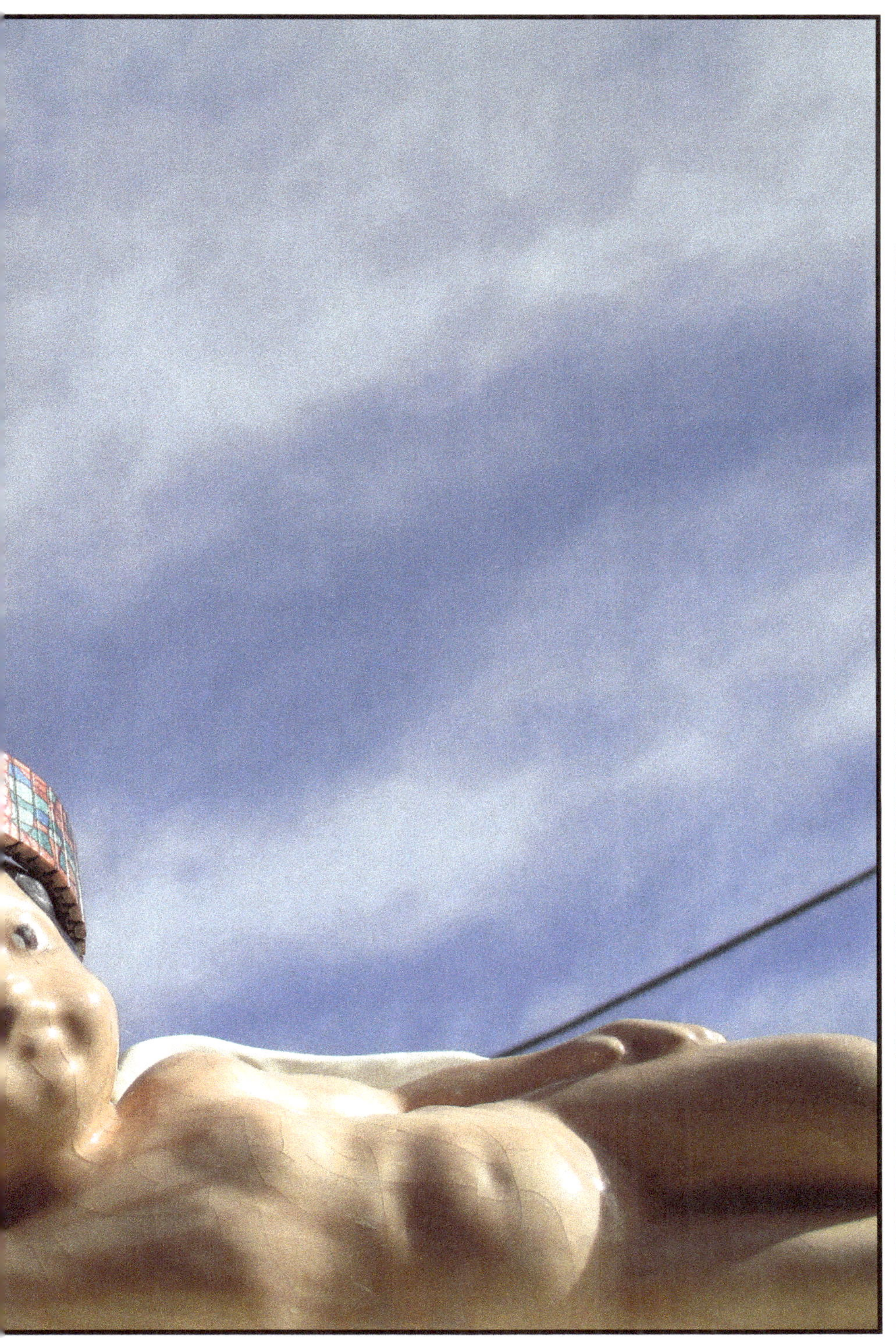

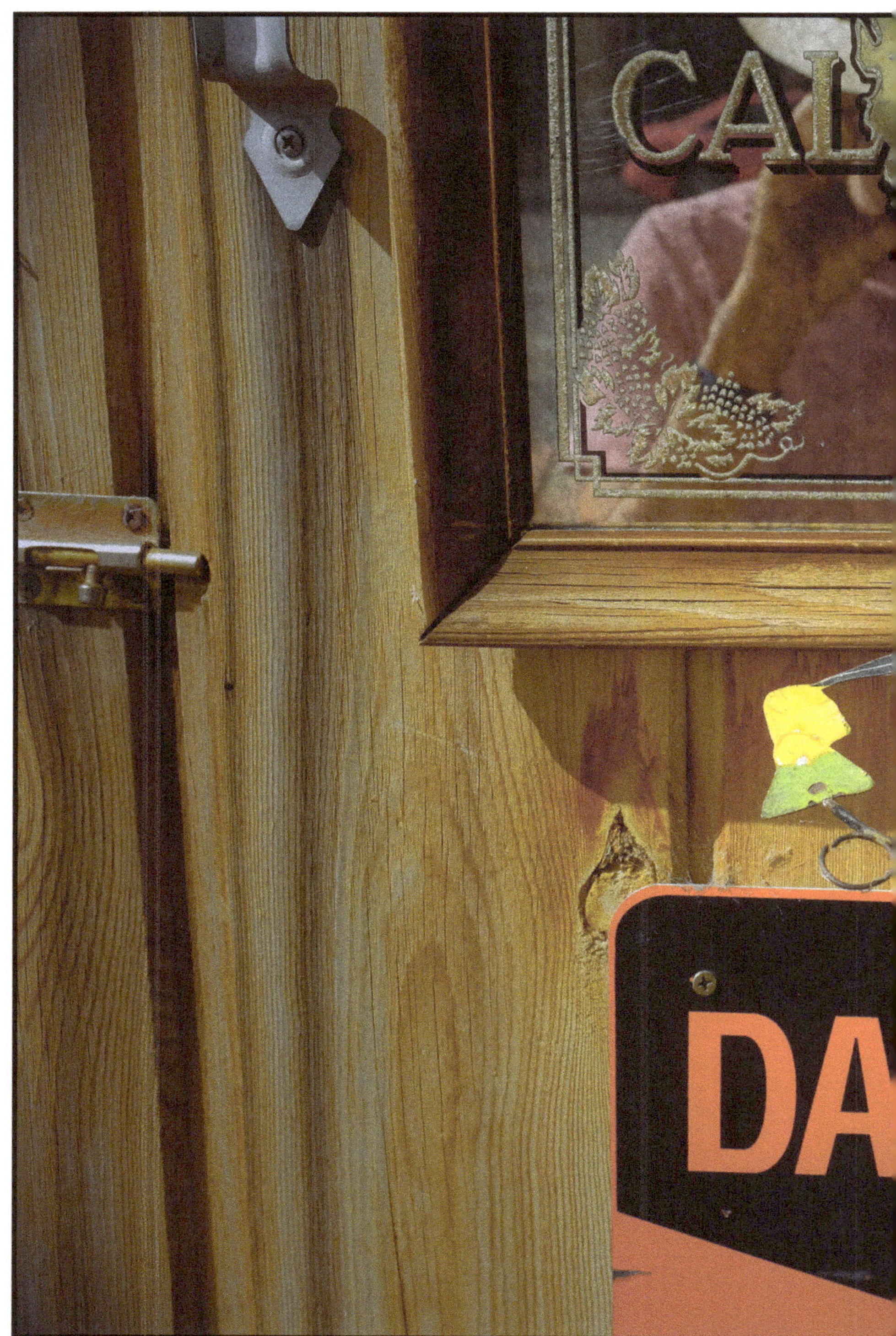

CAL
DA

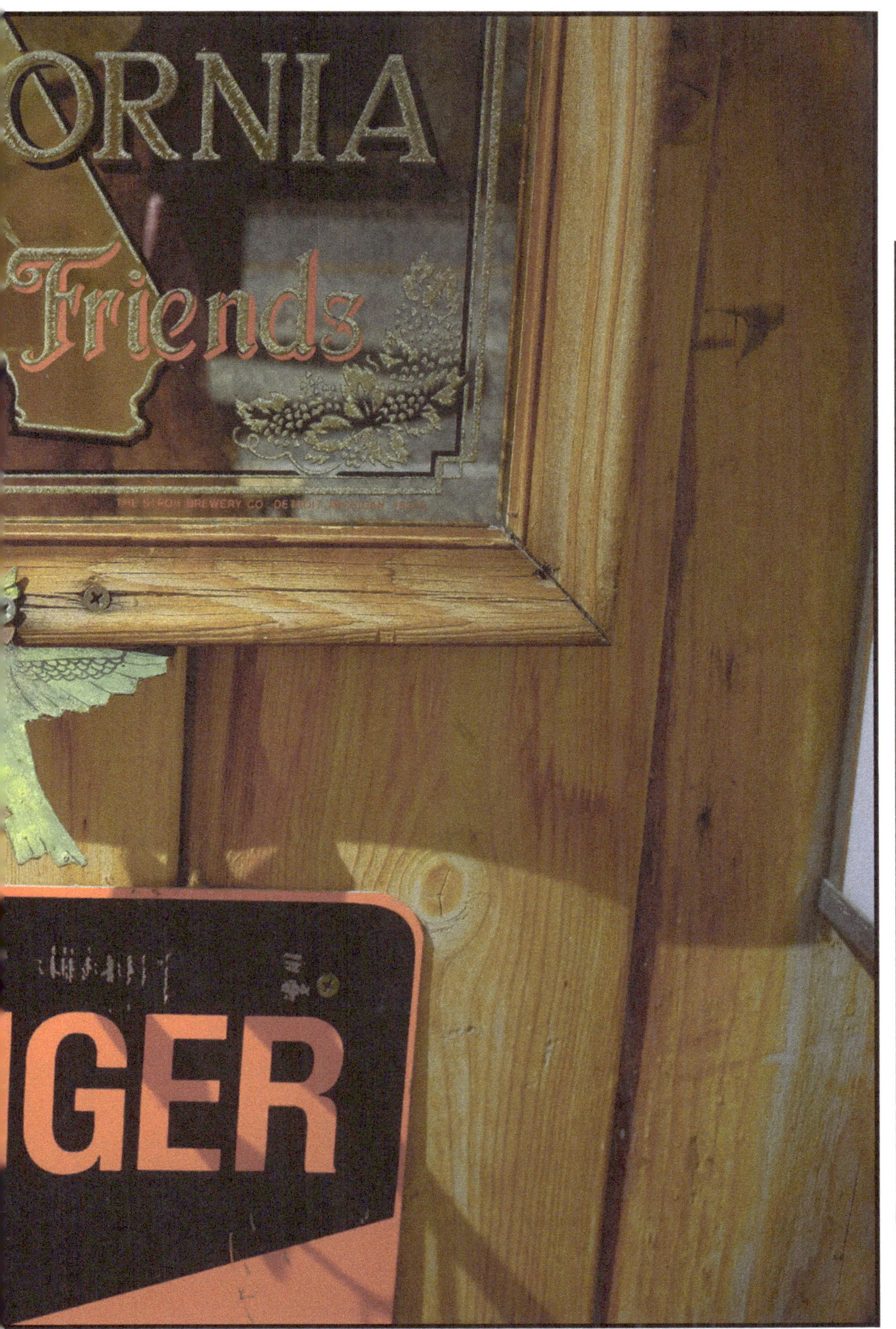
ORNIA
Friends
THE STROH BREWERY CO. DETROIT, MICHIGAN U.S.A.
GER

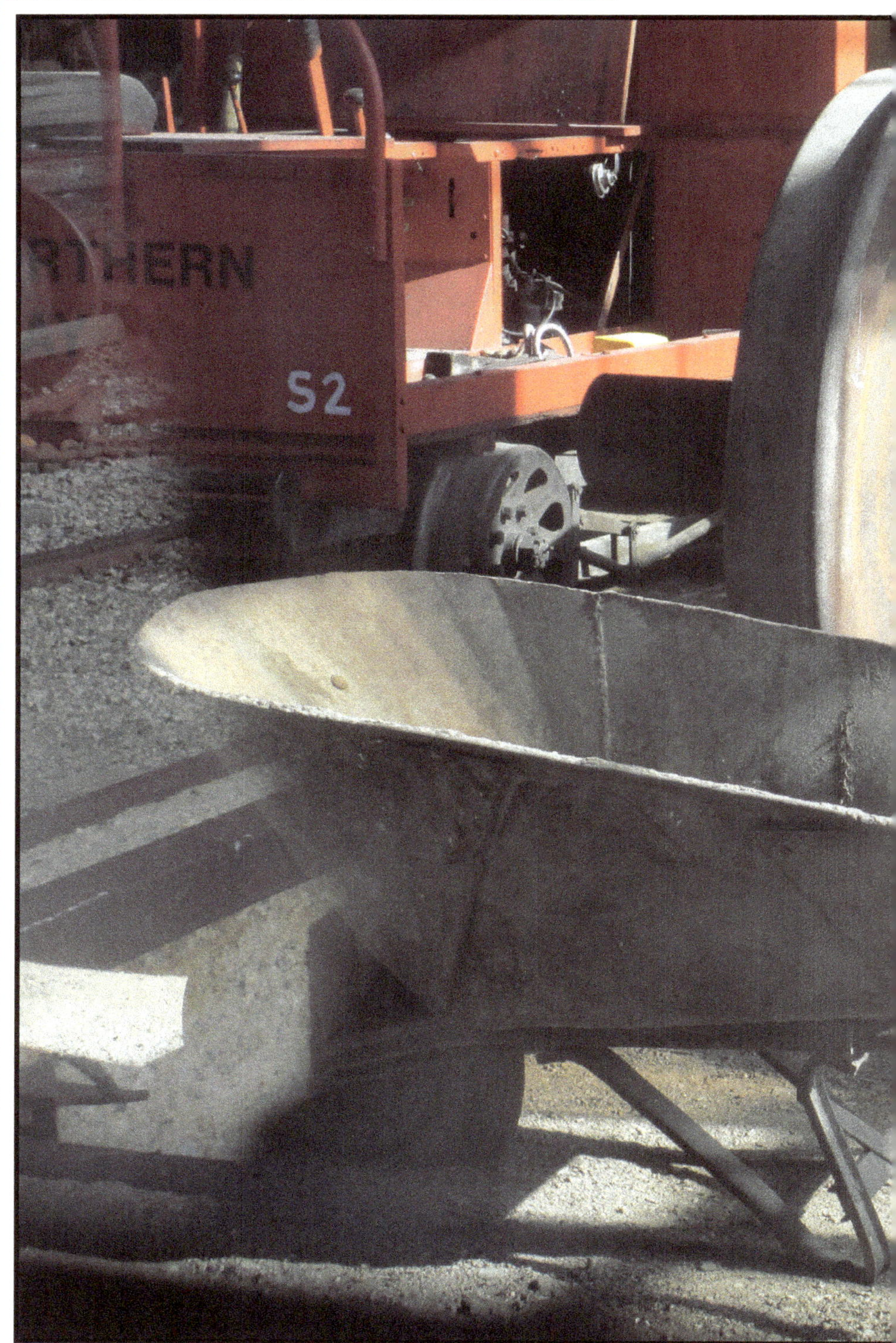
RTHERN
S2

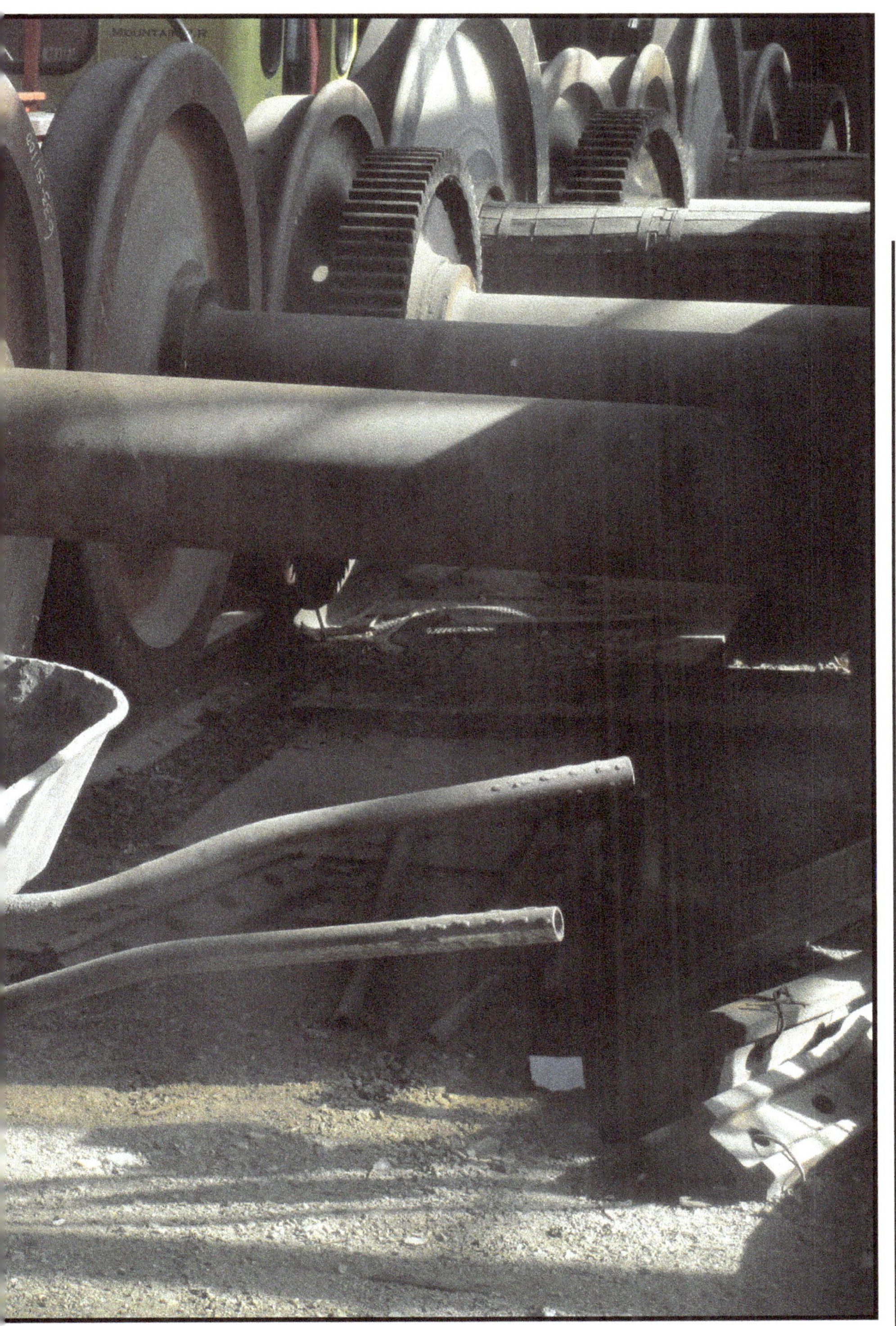

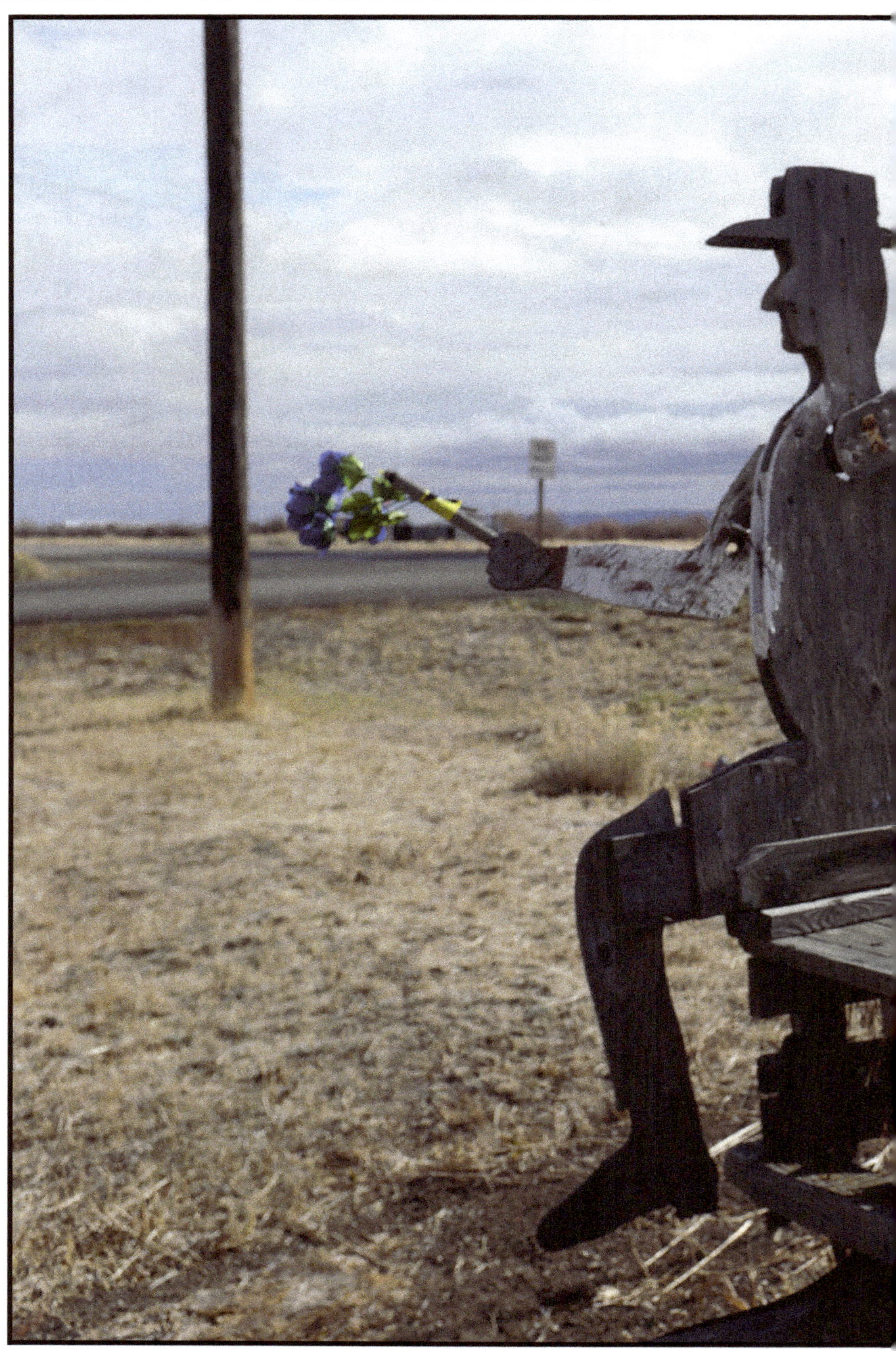

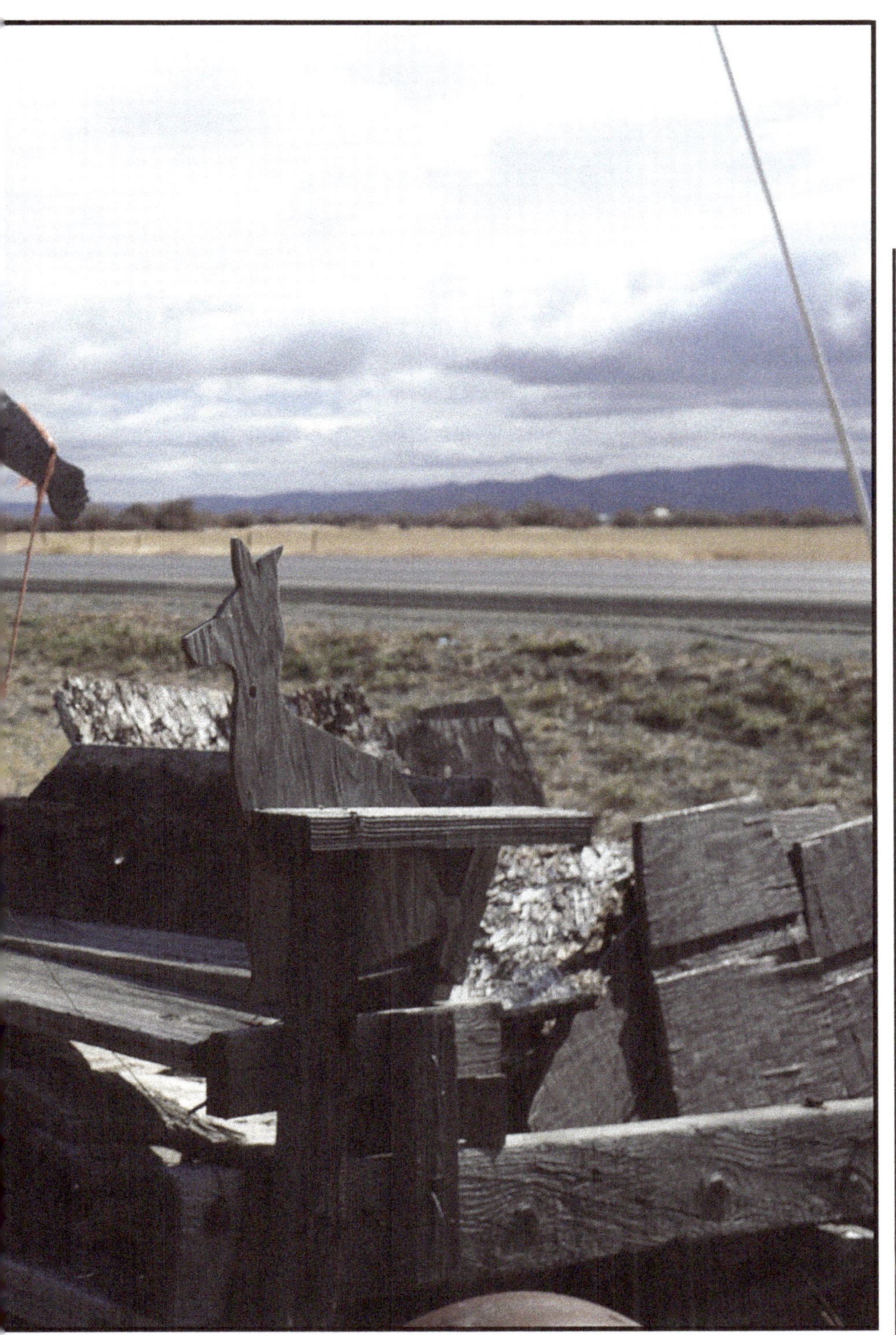

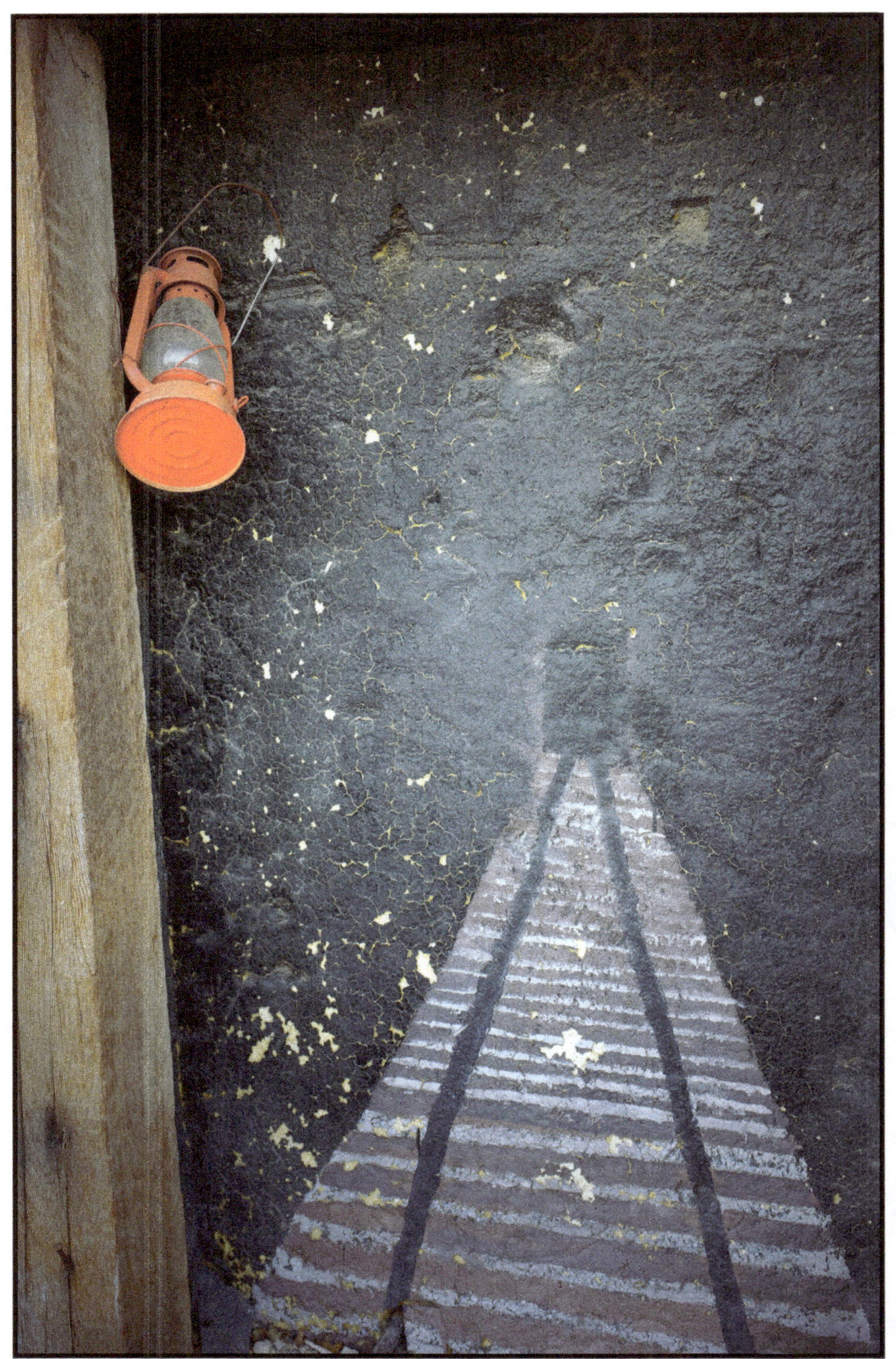

Waltz for Debby

Ryan Harper

To the sound of musicians at the watering places, there they repeat the triumphs of the Lord.

Twelve after nine circles
a June breeze, whisking
intervallic the lindenbloom
into my courtyard. Light
 but thick, honeyed morning
(for this touch with soft solids)
leaning back I'm listening
in the city to Debby's number:
alto from the highest window
unit droning awake
as her shade gives way,
blue and green,
below her the dish ping
and low brush loll,
fizzle of the patio
rinse and sweet broom
drawing back—cool of tenor
the dwellers riveted riding
out their tender chores,
inner voicings, inner court
relaxing matter
into motion, winging
around the lush base
of shared space.

THROWING NUMBERS

Ken Edward Rutkowski

I throw my number down and someone picks it up palms facing down picks it up from the ground with two hands stares at me from across the street walks back across smiling hands it to me with two hands palms facing up I say hello walk on number thrown down hands held together four hands a piece of paper four hands of relief of persistence across the street we acknowledge each other I see the broken street I see the leaf fall down the River and then wonder how it is that we all meet she comes across and says hello good day two hands facing up palms to the Sky we look each other in the eye let it go let it go easy for me to do not say easy for me to let it go not say gestures not words acknowledgement recognition lucky number or inevitable circumstance I'm a man standing across the road on the same line as Ho Chi Minh the lady looks at me and wonders why I don't take the money back she found it on the street the leaf floats down the River across the sunny Highland and with all this hassle without asking when the woman will be back we don't say Amen we say well fine.

Abstract Self

Megan Stephenson

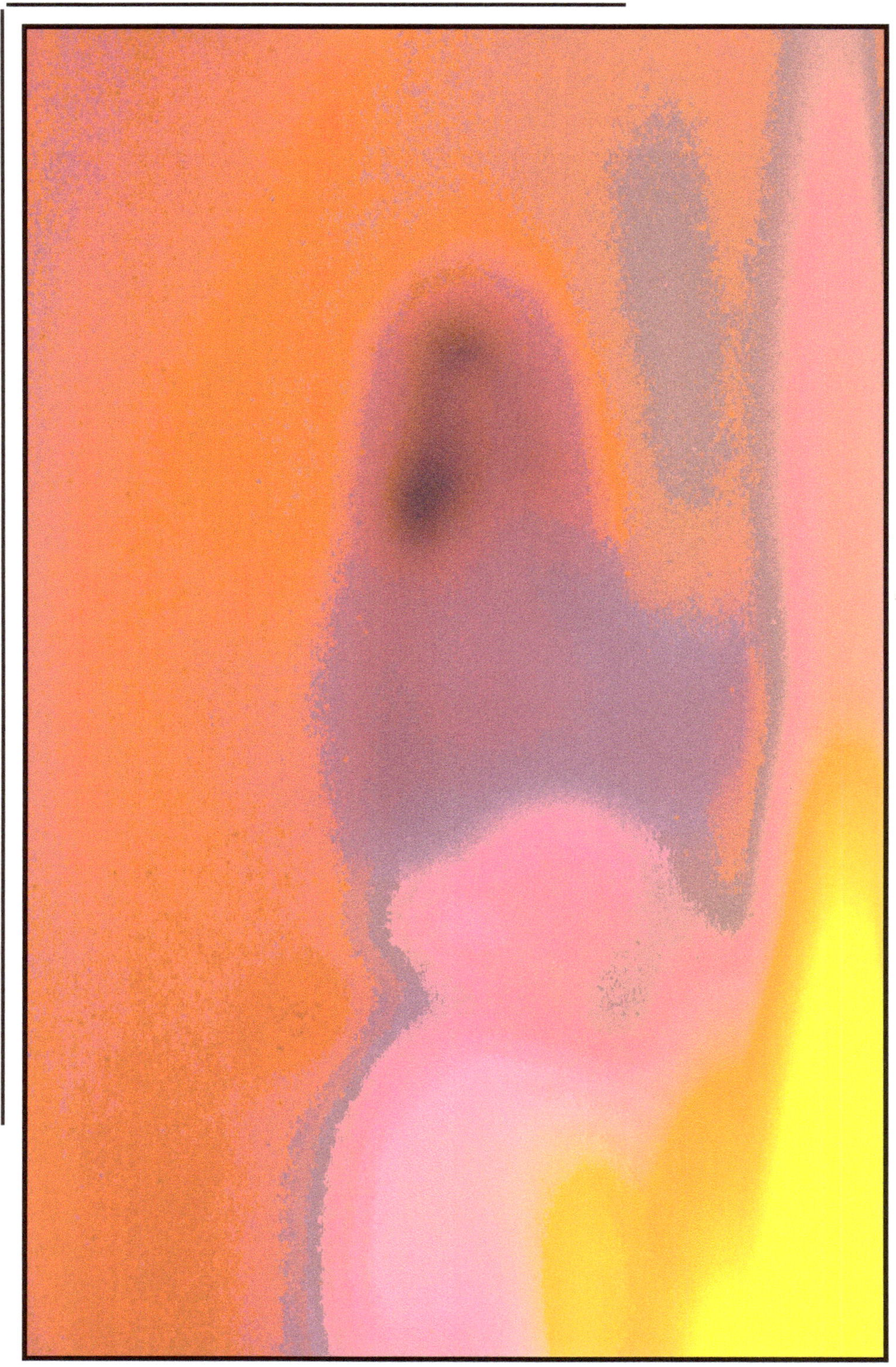

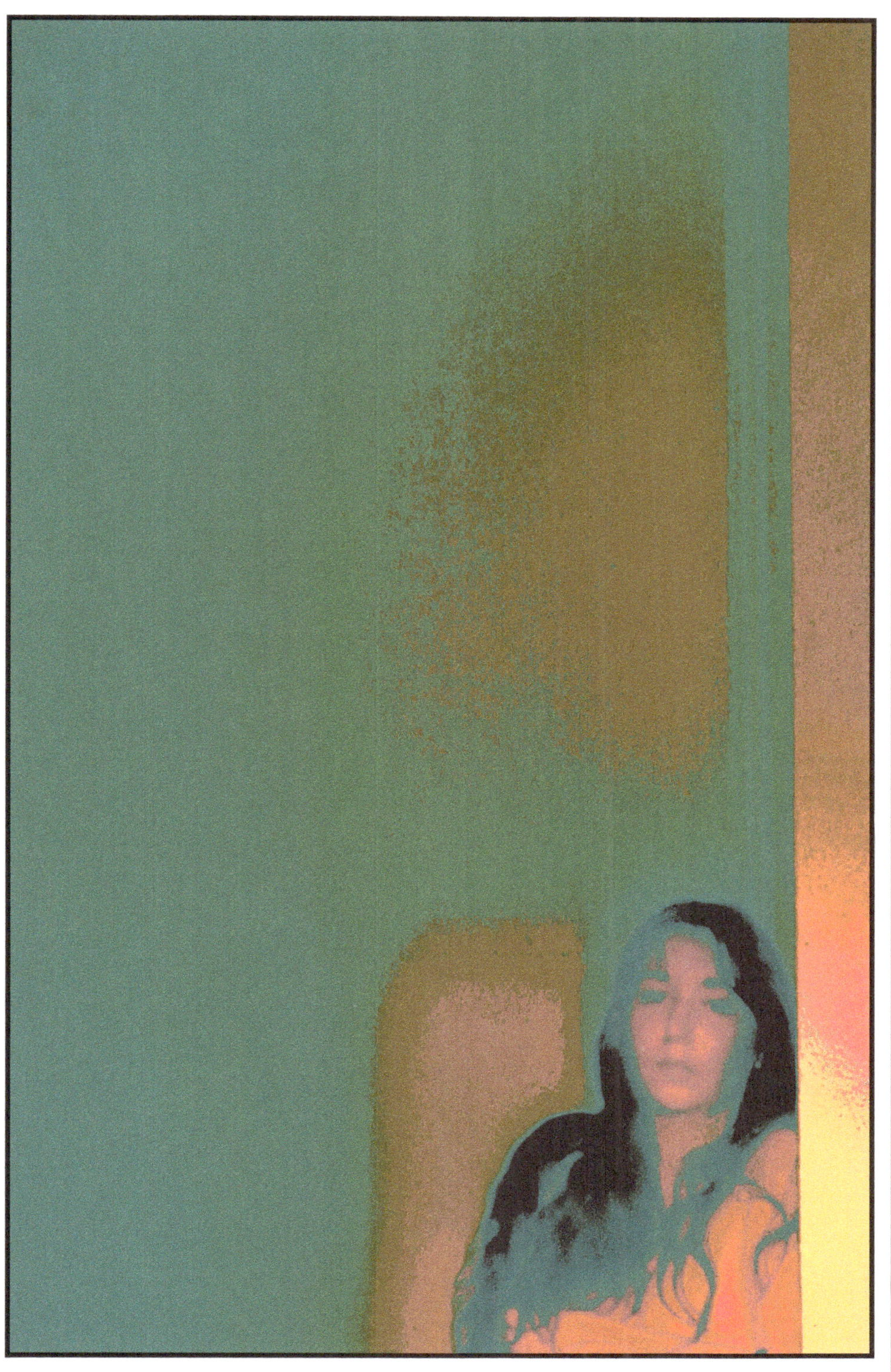

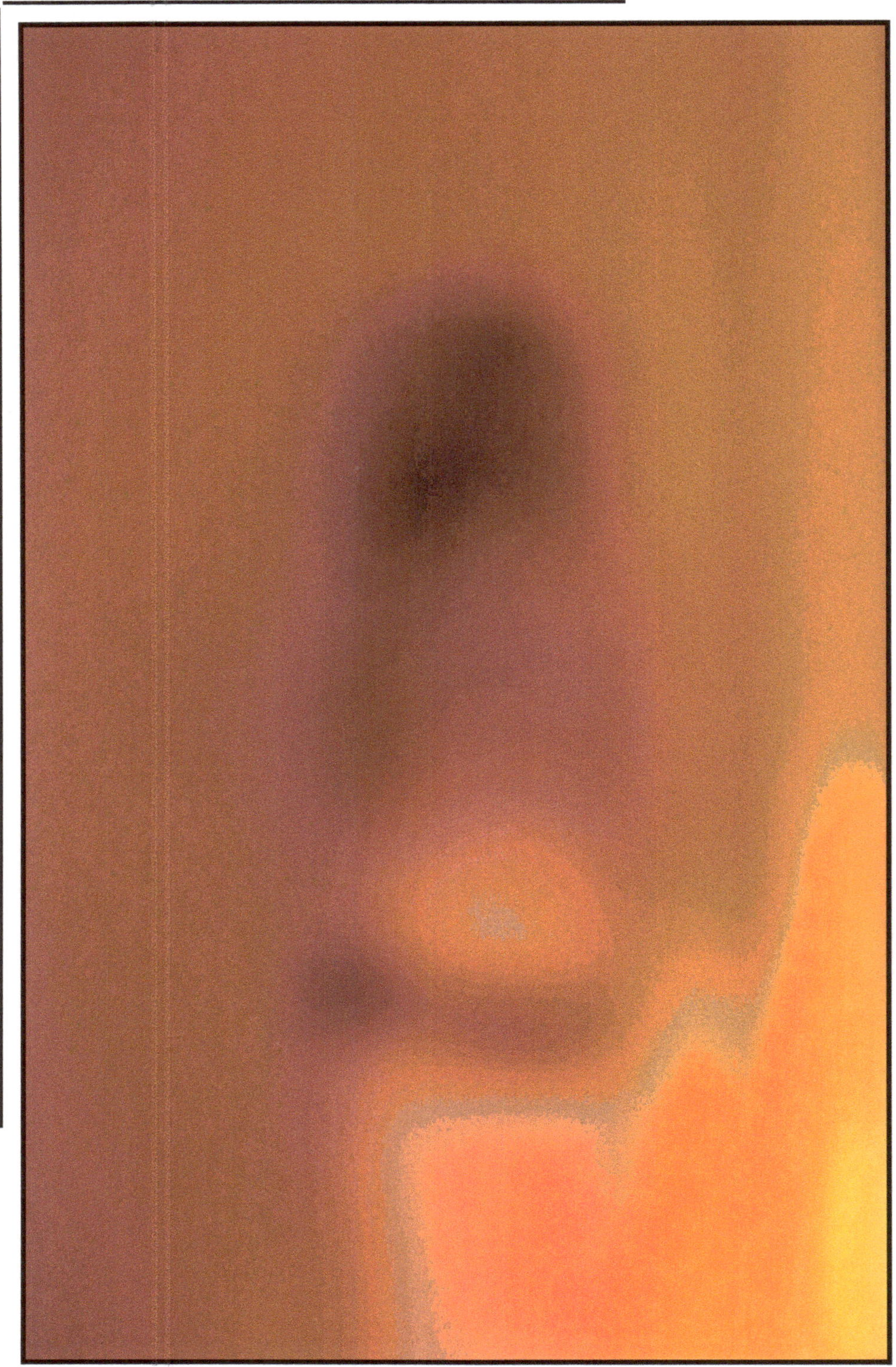

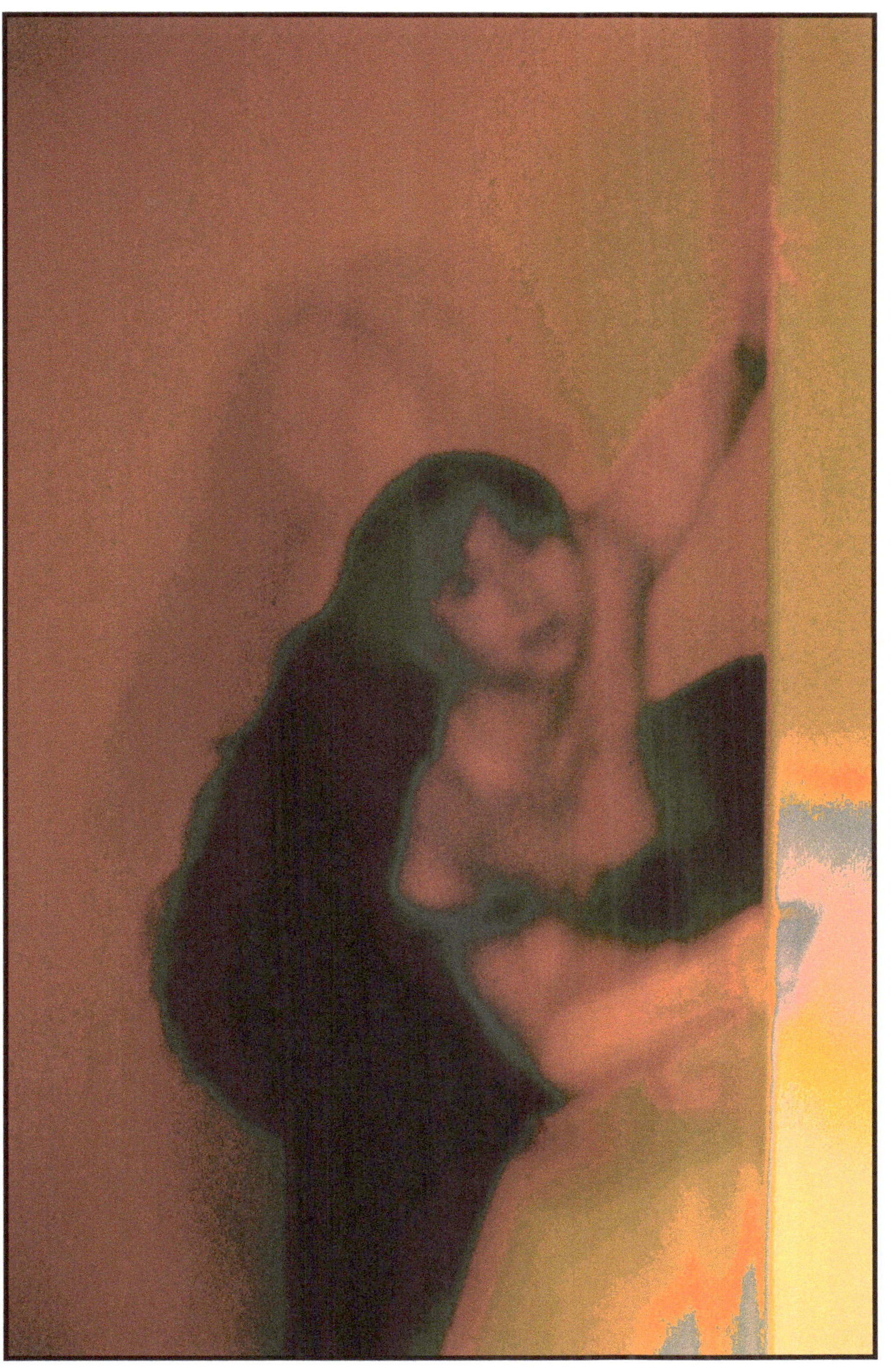

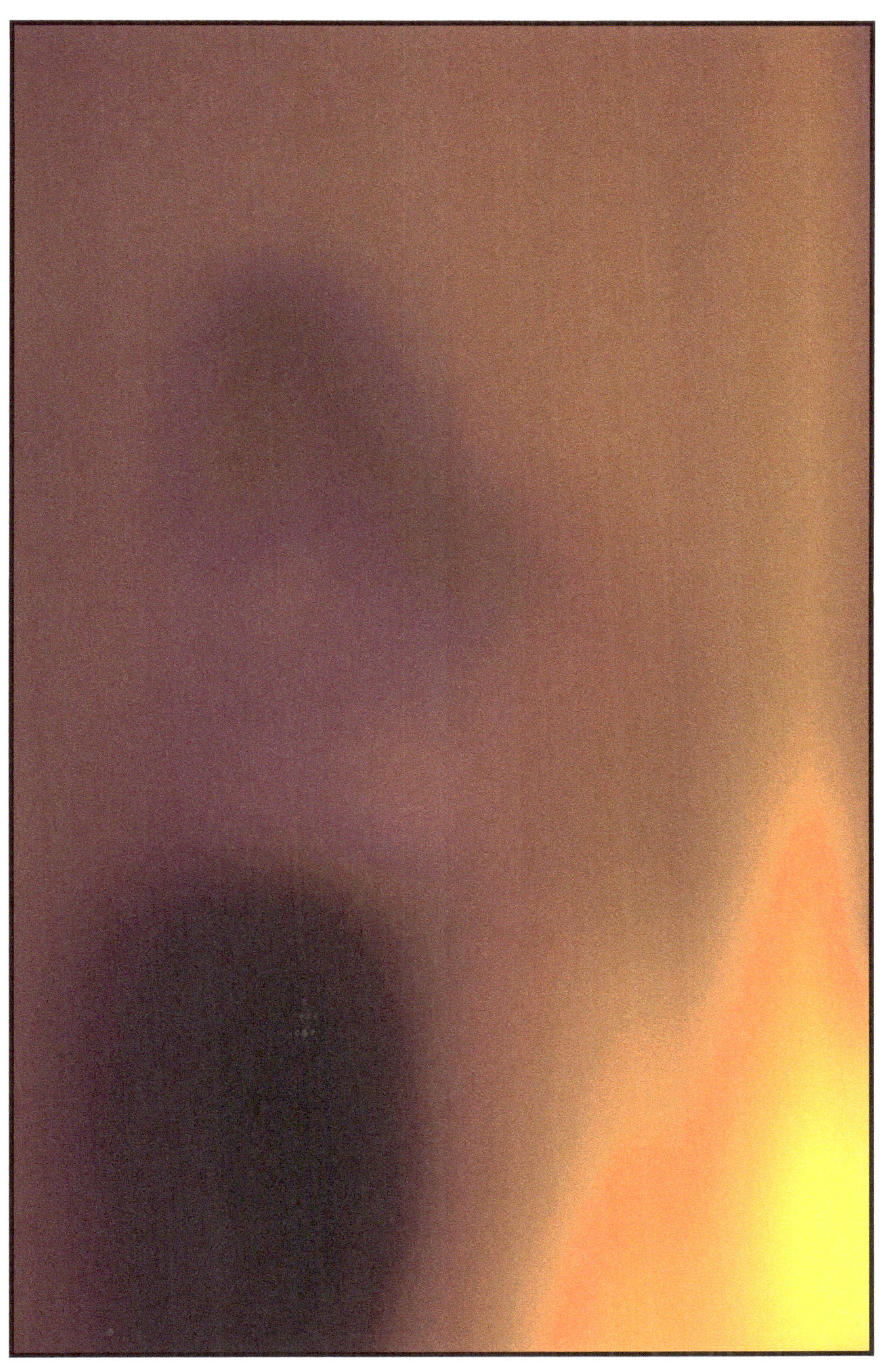

Staging Three Seasons for No Particular Reason

Cindy Patrick

Sundown ending the tropical, peach is rounding the violet lake

Boo, I just bought these cute flowy shorty-shorts, lost some weight,

found the right Jackie-O sunglasses to scrutinize fellow vacationers

stirring my last morning Caesar with pickled asparagus

Relax trout. Empty dock, grey so quiet, cottage shutters closed for bats to hide in

sand pails, volleyball net tucked into storage

Russet sunrise

Canning jars ready to fill with summer's fruity repast

cardigans lugged out of blanket chests, sleeves drag, shoulders slope

fluffy cranberry and pumpkin yarn to knit clumpy itchy neck things

flue checked for bird nests, jigsaw puzzles camp on the dining table now,

White arrives too soon. Feel the breath frost, screech of blue icicles

on metal door frames, barefoot on the frosty sidewalk retrieving the stiff litter

blown in, eyeballs feel like they may crack if I close my lashes

shiver so hard my teeth clack, fingers seem bruised

around an oversized mug of orange pekoe tea, tuck back in Grandma's feather bed

Muster point

cheeks sautéed after a diligent lube of SPF 60, strawberry nose

multiplying back freckles, herding together as bed fellows

awake under the lemon and blue umbrella, laser pinholes of the blazing sun

groggy, sticky sweat, a vinyl lounger, ants licking, tickling ankles

check warm beer cans for wasps, reaching cold end of a hose

to splash face, feet, pansies, and robins fly down to gulp in the mud,

emerald hummingbirds flit in and out

admire my crash-dieted, brassy figure in the patio glass,

thumbs up to watercress salads and cucumber water

just weeks left of refreshing play until maples turn gamboge

to rust, leaves loosen in surrender, blushing, escape
pride comes before Fall, as do we all

Everyday Heroes.

Mark Putzi

Grandma Seizure buzzes the skies over distressed Baltimore gripping tight the handles of her jet propelled walker patrolling rumors of a Supreme Boys rally choking ethnic neighborhoods with a supersized human swastika. In tow is the Muffinator, grasping in her powerful though tiny jaws a tremendous canvas bag.

"Look, Dearie, there it is!" GS nods, careful not to lose her grip on her means of transport and have to parachute in with her hearts and flowers oversized nightie. Below, the dark hate figure creeps slowly toward City Hall. "We'll crop dust em, Muffinator. Be ready!"

The shih tzu growls with half its mouth. Since she's been awarded full family status post her stint at the shelter, she's taken to GS and her new role as sidekick in their crusade to stamp out hate.

Below, the marchers compare riot gear. "Look brother. I've got the latest insert porcelain bulletproof knee guards and chest protector."

"Pretty cool. Got your Johnny Quest Arctic bear spray? Guaranteed effective to minus thirty?"

"Affirmative! What election was it we were fixing this time?"

"2032...In New York, they've got 28 and 24's at the Capitol."

"Wowza! This must be the coolest American Supreme Boy rally of all time! Three cities...Three separate radical takovers!"

GS cuts low through the ancient repurposed symbol's heart, emitting a con trail over St. Paul Street, as the Walters Art Museum cringes to her left, choked with Fascist stink. The swastika lurches East toward downtown. "Bomb's away, Muffinator!" Her tiny but powerful companion half-splits her vicious jaws, releasing piecemeal the deadly cargo.

"Look, brother! It's an old lady droppin food on us! You go Granny! White power! White power!"

Donuts coat the Fascists and are gobbled up like hotcakes. Magically they transform into hippies.

"Hey man, look what you're wearin'. Look what **I'm** wearin'. Oh Lord, get this off me!"

Elongated beards transpose to the tops of bald heads, emit lovingly, flowingly down to their backside beltlines. They top strip and bare chested wander off in search of tie dyes.

"There's a park, hey. C'mon, let's go pick flowers!"

II

Boss Toad practices looks of condescension in the mirror, squelching the urge to laugh and spoil the mood when he hits on a good one. He wants to keep his dress tidy, professional. His tattoo portrait of Ayn Rand disguises neatly beneath a suitcoat, along with his other shoulder, the one he calls Something Similar. He's one of the intelligencia, a phrenologist who focuses on physical manifestations of Manifest Destiny. The bumps on your head will tell you who deserves and who don't. Black? Don't count on recognition. Native American? You know your place. Erased from history like the phantom hand you dig for gold with to give Columbus. Boss Toad will tell you all that sword wielding, skull smashing just an attempt bring phrenology more in tow with reality. And speaking of forensics, he's in league with the top cops, the moneyed underbelly of the mayor's office. Boss Toad envisions himself a puppeteer, the man behind the curtain pulling levers, choking the room with steam and cigar stink. He loves a good Cuban as long as he's subservient. But on the surface, a good PR man is so PC: money to be made pushing Rainbow Coalitions. And in the process of tearing them down, a sustainable audience. A good guy and a bad guy can be the same guy depending on perspective.

In communication with city planners, he's paved the way for a massive demonstration from the Milkweed Coalition, promoting the absolute necessity of order by whatever necessary means. Their emblem is a powerfully knuckled white fist holding a bunch of weeds gone to seed, a parody of a Woodstock promotion sans a bird of peace flying concomitant. Each sports a dirk in a calf holster. They like to compare lengths and sharpening methods, pass between themselves anatomical drawings with structures best to penetrate exed out in red. For bigger jobs, they have artillery.

Intimidate to win! their motto. Boss Toad likens it to planting a flag on the moon. No one knows the value of an undercurrent puppet master. Then in '28 with complete control, the value becomes apparent. You see, you build a building from the bottom up. You hang the structure, raise the architectural steel, leave off the flashing and fascia till people grow comfortable with its looks, then **BOOM!** Suddenly our adversaries never vote again! The cause of good becomes the cause of us inseparably. Boss Toad is so proud the mirror seems even to be proud of him.

He makes a phone call. "Secretary Daily? Get me Eunice!" Instantly Eunice acknowledging his clout. "Hey Baby! We set for tomorrow?"

"Tomorrow and every day," Eunice exclaims. "Toad, you are the best, the most benevolent of all masters."

"I concur," concurs the Toadster, "You know how they tried to usurp our pride? They didn't."

Eunice replies, "They can have whatever self-satisfaction limited success can get you."

"Long as we're the ones who set the limits," Toad completes the thought.

III

The Kittycam identifies the doorstep. Trained in surveillance, she scratches first at the corner of the door which the Toadster opens, swipes at her with his boot. After three days of continued pestering, his heart, like Jesus, rises and he sets out a saucer of milk. Another two days, and she runs inside when the door cracks. She's softened him, made him believe in love among demagogues.

"I'll call you Toadie," he tells her, notes the midnight darkness of her coat, "It'll play well with swing voters while they still can." The Kittycam reveals a world known only to elite Capitalists. Busts and a drawing room. Busts and a rotunda. A bust at the elbow of a circular staircase. At the end of a hall littered with portraiture a kitchen with a chef dressed all in white. She rubs her head and the side of her body into the Toadster's shins.

Access Kittycorder captures covert Toadstool conspiracy permeating office of the comptroller YouTube bound. Feeds interrupting routine worka-days in city and state governments with pop-ups. "What you mean permit de-nied! This is BS. We're set to march in one week! OK listen, maybe Wall Street is too much push. Howbout anywhere in Manhattan? Greenwich Village, Soho, even Brooklyn. Even Harlem, for Crissakes!" Toadster's consternation visible on closed circuit, sweat pooling in the bags turkeynecking his eyes. "What? Even Soho a no go? Jesus!"

"Look maestro," answers a voice heavily electrified, later unscramble to i.d. the comptroller. "You never talked to me. You don't know me. Drop your fucking IPhone in the Hudson. And don't dial this number again till you ferret out your mole!"

IV

In DC evil is customary. Communication travels electronically, over ever-expanding frequencies. Underground, they develop a discourse, and when their language breaks the surface, they understand it in nuance. The in**SIN**uation. The dogooders did it, taught the bad boys how to borrow it. Now everyone says something, means something else. The word ubiquitous has lost its meaning, because everything means something frequent as the word the. Washington has aged in what's still a young country, literally with its messen-gers, figuratively with its re-invention of the re-invention of the wheel. It's a self-obsessed city, skewed Left, but unwilling to **Right**fully despise. We need each other, Washington believes, as if they were all human at the same time. But unseemingly one parasitizes, the other plays host. The city lacks symbiosis as they kill themselves trying tolive.

Workman is a Christian DJ justifying violence. When you hold some-thing to be self-evident, it implies historically you've told the truth. Workman is a firebrand. For him, the truth's not arbitrary, it's invented to belabor opinions. "Man, you gotta know this. I appeal to your inner self, the self you know and feel and express at night when you wake up shaking! A starving man can point his finger all he wants, but at the end of the day, unless he uses that finger to plant a tomato or some goddam thing, he's still starving." Workman's an iconoclast who's moved into Phase II, post indoctrination. "We've got to make them understand. The way to do it is to raise hell!" he shouts into the microphone. "We deserve a voice!" Only he won't explain what qualifications he owns to mantle up. "I won't be silenced! I'll shout for that which is, for that which has been, so perfect! And so fragile! Think of your kids at night! Think of them, what they're hearing! Do they deserve this? Everywhere in this town... All we see is an abuse of power!" He explains they gather in darkness, set fire to living animals. He's seen them rejoicing over the pain, heartlessly extoling every king of blurst humanity en masse. A Conspiracy! In the daylight, they don their false masks, try to convince us what's good for us, but **LO!** We know what we see. We have eyes! They insult our intelligence claiming honesty!

The demonstration will assemble peacefully. A few will know, but not one who will be martyred. There can't be any leaks. "Understand the importance of what you do when you gather here," Workman explains. "Have faith in what you do. God's work is sometimes difficult. Think of how you'll change the world, and your reward, both here and in heaven!"

He's been selling them for weeks. Now they're sold. Like a box of old tin soldiers bought cheap, you assume they'll accrue in value. One day, you'll have a fortune, but now you have to take the first step. Workman has a qualification: He sold timeshares.

"Man, listen to me. I'm imploring you! I understand your frustration. Now's your chance to give it voice! We're meeting X place and X time and X is what we want! You don't show up and you're a coward. That's all I'm saying."

In three weeks' time, they intend to ruin the Democracy in 2024. They want you begging for a dictator, not merely accepting one. They don't want you scared to death, but scared to reticence. The dead are useless, good for nothing but mulch.

"I've never seen such unbridled enthusiasm," Workman blathers from his tiny studio. His producer outside his soundproof enclosure is all thumbs up! The infomercials rage for fifteen minutes while his audience cringes, suffers the little death inside, waiting for resolution, closure. In the end, he gives them permission. Tune in tomorrow. He'll give them permission again.

The opposition with a soul cannot plant a bomb there, at his Workman Place. The opposition with a soul locked in strategy to disarm the narrative. "If we say nothing, we support him. If we speak out, he asserts his freedom to incite." Part of his fame is they want to kill him, everyone opposing. They can't say it or not, every way increasing his power. They're waiting at his house, a counterdemonstration. Some have snuck inside. This isn't questionable right of resistance. This is breaking and entering. But do they see a choice? They must enter his mind, and to do that they sequester his body.

He comes home and looks for his dog. It's well fed and muzzled in the closet, sleeping. He strips, enters the shower, blasts the shame off him. They're inside now, crowding him. "What? What? Wait a minute, what? Who are you, what?"

"We're your conscience, Workman," they explain. "We want you to think what did you contribute to this world."

"Man, get away from me!" He tries pushing through, but they grab and impede, despite his slippery skin. "Oh my god! Help! Help!" The neighbors hear his cries, but understand who he is. They help him just as much as he has bothered to help them. He continues to scream until they have subdued him, brought him to the ground. This had once been a gated community. Now, with the padlocks removed, every resident is subject to the ancient times, the hunter-gatherers. He begins to cry as he lay subdued on the cold tile of his bathroom, steam hovering above him, obscuring most, masking those who've secured him. Then, one by one, they kiss him on his top set of cheeks. When finished, they explain they suspect he has a soul.

The next day, Workman doesn't show up for work. In a week's time he's out looking for a job. He winds up a line cook at Denny's. Several times a day, he has to go to the walk-in cooler to shed his tears.

Workman is eventually replaced by an even louder DJ. However, lacking sufficient following, the date of the promised violent demonstration fades and dies away like a flower gone to seed.

78

Am I languishing, burnt out, or do I need MDMA?

Arthur Tarley

Gosh, I've been feeling bummed during the pandemic. Ya, know? Spending hours sitting in the dark, refreshing doge. Eating bowlfuls of par-boiled cauliflower. Going days wearing the same skid marked undies.

Naturally, I turned to news headlines for help. *"Are you burnt out?" "Raise your hand if you're burnt out." "Do you smell toast?"* My hand did not raise and I did not smell toast. Hence, I concluded I was not burnt out.

A friend texted me an article about how the word "languishing" had come to define some of the downtrodden during the isolating pandemic. Then, I thought about some delicious langostino I had one time off the southern tip of Italia. I pondered aloud, "Could I be languishing if I was delighted by such a delicious memory of langostino?" It was only one memory, yet it was so delicious. I finally determined while dining on langostino ceviche from the local latin restaurant, Lucia's, that I was not languishing.

sat back down on my ever-so-slightly soiled underwear and pondered… "What's going on with me? And why isn't the answer in any of these self-help articles?"

Then, I stumbled across an interesting line of royal blue letters in my browser window. *"Are you hopeless?"* it read. "That could be it," I pondered. I clicked. It was a questionnaire. I felt like I was on to something.

"Are you binge eating?" Does cauliflower count?

"Do you have an appetite?" I just said I was binge eating cauliflower.

"Are you having trouble falling asleep?" Yes.

"Are you having trouble staying asleep?" Yes.

"Are you having trouble getting back to sleep?" Well, I can fall back to sleep after eating a PB&J and re-watching two episodes of *Selling Sunset.* Is that "trouble?"

"Do you feel sluggish during the day?" Only when I run out of peanut butter.

"Do you drink enough water?" No.

"How's your sex drive?" Average.

"Do you exercise regularly?" I do the down part of push-ups most days. Not the ups, just the downs.

"Do you feel like you lack control over your life?" On a personal level: not really. Well, a little. But the Deep State has far more unaccountable control over my life than I do, in a broader sense.

"Do you have persistent concerns about the Deep State?" Yes.

"When you hear the word 'deep' what's the next word that comes to mind?" Dish.

"Do you have issues with short-term memory?" I don't think so.

"Do you have trouble falling asleep?" Didn't you already ask that?

"Maybe you're having issues with your short-term memory." Yeah, maybe.

So, I was answering a lot of questions on this mental health diagnostic survey from The Daily Digestive, but what was it all for? Well, when I pressed submit, it said, *"You're depressed. Very depressed. You've likely been depressed for a very long time. You've probably even tried antidepressants, and they didn't help, right? You need something stronger. MDMA is the answer. Unfortunately, you'd have to get into some exclusive clinical trial to try it out. Or go black market, of course. Does this help?"* I almost threw up my langostino ceviche!

Everyday Nativity Scene

Photography by John Lightle

Poetry by David Capps

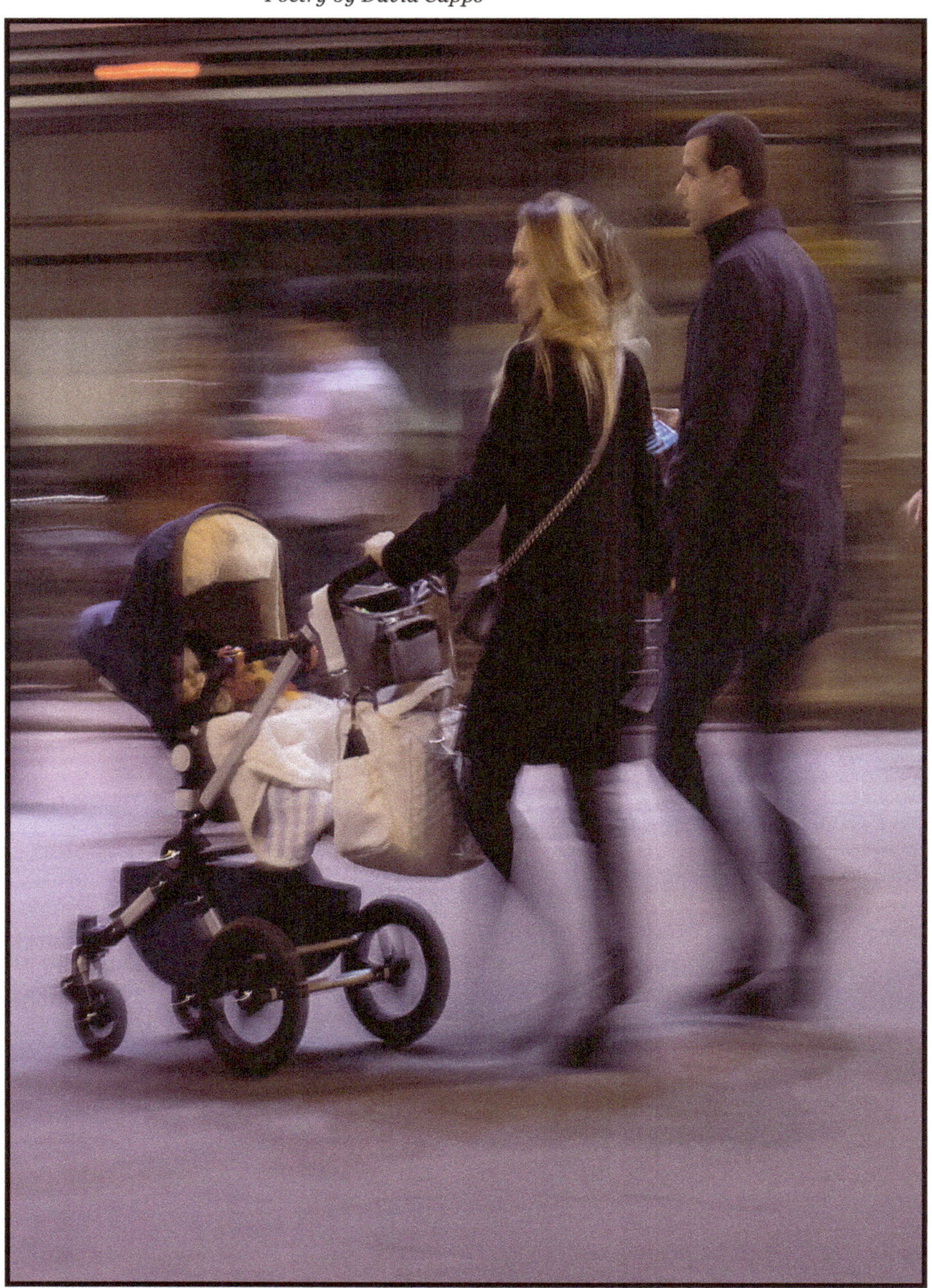

Rushing to catch their flight
the baby snug in his hearse
the man's hand preoccupied
with some cell phone game

they will be late. In the blur
of God's lab coat enfolding
them, the families staying in
the hotel room, the airport

and its meccas, and nature
collecting around God, water
beads at the mindless edge
of the petri dish, displaced.

If you could play it backward
the billions and billons served
would starve down to a point
and there would be bliss—

there ugliness would stare
into the loneliness of space.

In Order Of Appearance:

Roger Craik is English by birth and educated at British universities, and live in Ashtabula, Ohio. His poems have been published in England, Australia and America, in translation in Bulgaria, Romania, and Belarus, and he has written four full-length books of poetry, of which the most recent is Down Stranger Roads (2014). A new book, In Other Days, is in press.

Sydney Yount's art-making is bound by spirituality, alternate realms, manifestations, and the link of chaos between the micro and macro of this universe. Her own queer nature draws her to bright colors, loud and delicate noises, and textures. Through becoming an educator she has become quite the critic of institutions, government, and the world at large, while remaining ever-confident there's more. sydneyyount.com

April Rubasch received her MFA in creative writing with an emphasis in poetry from the University of Arizona in 2005. She was the recipient of the Fred N. Scott Award for fiction and the M.P. Hamilton Award for poetry through the University of Arizona and was nominated for the Ruth Lily Poetry Prize. Her poetry has been featured in Into the Teeth of the Wind, High Shelf Press, and Poet's Choice, and her fiction has been featured in the Writer's Digest and and will be featured in The Stardust Review.

For as long as she can remember, Emily has kept sketchpads and notebooks, filled with the pages of her life, in words and images.
She loves finding one of her past books and flipping through it.
There is both surprise and familiarity in what she finds inside.
The poems, and the pictures, transport her right back to where she was and how she felt, the day she wrote or sketched them.
They are evocative, in so many ways.
They remind her of moments of her life, sometimes joyful, sometimes painful, and occasionally they surprise her by recalling the depth of feeling she experienced, and the strange recognition of herself, ,as she was then, changed over the years, but the same in many ways.
She will always write, and draw and paint. It is her way of expressing deep joy, terrible sadness, or just the strange and wonderful and agonising and beautiful aspects of being alive.
It has always been a very private part of her life, until now.
She has not felt brave enough to expose herself, the most secret, real ways she sees the world, and feels about life, or about herself.
However, she has long hoped to create a book which, like one of her sketchpads, is an intriguing and exciting, thought provoking, visual and verbal feast , which, perhaps would be as interesting to others, as looking through her sketchpads and the wealth of thoughts and feelings they provoke is, to her.
She hopes it might inspire emotion, stir the senses, perhaps prompt recognition of certain feelings or experiences.she hopes it moves people, and makes them thoughtful.
So, here they are....some of her poems, in this case...private for so many years...her heart and soul on paper.
She hopes they make people feel.

Min Ji Park was born in South Korea and raised in Hong Kong. She attended New York University but has since moved back to Hong Kong. Although she worked with film photography for a few years, she has been more consistent when she began using it to help with symptoms of her Autism Spectrum Disorder. In addition to photography, she writes poetry and has been published in Poets Choice.

Corinne Hughes was born in the hill country of central Texas and currently resides in Portland, Oregon, where she works in community outreach at Portland State University. In 2004, she had the pleasure of attending the National Book Foundation Summer Writing Camp in Bennington, Vermont at the age of nineteen. After years working in conservation, Corinne went on to study in Russia and Kyrgyzstan during her undergrad. She worked as a freelance writer and received the Jury Prize in an

academic journal for her research abroad. In recent years, she has found her passion in literary arts nonprofit management and received an MPA from Portland State University. She continues to study with literary arts organizations, such as Catapult, Literary Arts, Write Around Portland, and The Attic. She is a 2021 participant of the One Story Writing Circle, an inaugural year-long education and accountability group hosted and moderated by One Story.
Instagram handle: @oleacae

Jose Varghese is a bilingual writer and translator from India. He is the author of 'Silver Painted Gandhi and Other Poems' and his short story manuscript 'In/Sane' was a finalist in the 2018 Beverly International Prize. His second collection of poems is scheduled for publication in 2021 by Black Spring Press Group, UK. He was a finalist in the London Independent Story Prize (LISP), a runner up in the Salt Prize, and was commended in the Gregory O'Donoghue International Poetry Prize. His works have appeared or are forthcoming in Joao Roque Literary Journal, SPLASH! (Haunted Waters Press), Bluing the Blade (Tempered Runes Press), Cathexis Northwest Press, Beyond Words Literary Magazine, The Best Asian Short Story Anthology, Dreich, Meridian – The APWT Drunken Boat Anthology of New Writing, Afterwards, Summer Anywhere, I Am Not a Silent Poet, Spilling Cocoa Over Martin Amis, Kavya Bharati, Bengaluru Review, Muse India, Re-Markings, Unthology 5, Unveiled, Reflex Fiction, Flash Fiction Magazine, Chandrabhaga, and Postcolonial Text.
Instagram : josevarghese101

Cree Cullars is a Black Queer emerging writer and artist from the South Side of Chicago.

Jodie West is a poet with a degree in English Literature from Claremont Mckenna College. She is currently an elementary school science teacher. Jodie has been published in the literary journal Humana Obscura. She lives in California with her multicultural family.

Mark Christopherson is a writer and attorney working in the Minneapolis area. He has published work most recently in The Dewdrop and Passengers Journal.

Cueva is a Cuban American woman from San Diego, California. She is currently pursuing her Master's in Creative Writing from Harvard University. Her writings work to break down barriers between the known and the foreign, all with the feminist mindset of providing accessibility and opportunity to all. By trade and education, she is a writer, folklorist, and cultural anthropologist. Read more at andreacuevaauthor.com

Roger Camp is the author of three photography books including the award-winning Butterflies in Flight, Thames & Hudson, 2002 and Heat, Charta, Milano, 2008. His documentary photography has been awarded the prestigious Leica Medal of Photography. His photographs are represented by the Robin Rice Gallery, NYC. His work has appeared in The New England Review, Southwest Review, Chicago Review and the New York Quarterly. More of his work may be seen at Luminous-Lint.com.

Ryan Harper is a Visiting Assistant Professor in Colby College's Department of Religious Studies. He is the author of My Beloved Had a Vineyard, winner of the 2017 Prize Americana in poetry (Poetry Press of Press Americana, 2018). Some of his recent poems and essays have appeared in Change Seven, Tahoma Literary Review, Wild Roof Journal, Spoon River Poetry Review, Cimarron Review, Chattahoochee Review, and elsewhere. Ryan is the creative arts editor of American Religion Journal.

Ken Edward Rutkowski lives in Ho Chi Minh City, Vietnam. His work has appeared in The Fiction Pool, Tofu Ink Arts Press (Summer 2021), Synchronized Chaos, The Journal of Experimental Fiction (#50), Fiction International (Fall 2021), Paragraph Line, Fiction Daily, Thieves Jargon and Borders: An Anthology of Whatcom County Writers. While in Asia, he has traveled around Vietnam, Cambodia, Taiwan, Indonesia, Malaysia, the Philippines, Borneo and Sri Lanka.

Megan Stephenson is a working artist located in Boston MA. She specializes in mixed media art, inclusive of painting, photography, and the mixing of both. She focuses on her sense of identity and the struggle to perform to societal standards, and cope with the strains of life as a disabled, queer and female identifying person. The photos she has submitted here, are demonstrative of her fluidity in self expression, and how her self expression is a constant flowing self realization, abstracted by the ideas and labels we put on eachother. If you wish to view more of her work you may follow her on instagram @art_by_megans.

Cindy lives in the Sooke, BC Canada rainforest and cashiers at a grocery store for fodder and to interrupt introversion. She is a product of her observations and the tenacious need to empty her head. Cindy's poems appear in Blank Spaces, Art and Word by Sooke Arts Council, and submits fiction online.

Mark Putzi received an MA in Creative Writing from the University of Wisconsin -- Milwaukee in 1990. He has published fiction and poetry in numerous small press and online venues in the U.S. and in other countries. His most recent publication, the short story "It's Rush Hour," appears in the blog In Parentheses in Spring of 2021. He lives in Milwaukee and works as a retail pharmacist.

Arthur Tarley is a writer and activist originally from Queens, New York. His work has appeared in Vox, Current Affairs, Jacobin, The Dillydoun Review, and Coffin Bell Journal.

John Lightle is a writer and photographer spending many hours sitting on his woodpile contemplating. While away from his frame shop, he drags his artwork among many area art shows. The job takes him across the countryside, and occasionally overseas, photographing the quiet resolve found within the golden hours.

David Capps is a philosophy professor and poet who lives in New Haven, CT. He is the author of three chapbooks: Poems from the First Voyage (The Nasiona Press, 2019), A Non-Grecian Non-Urn (Yavanika Press, 2019), and Colossi (Kelsay Books, 2020).

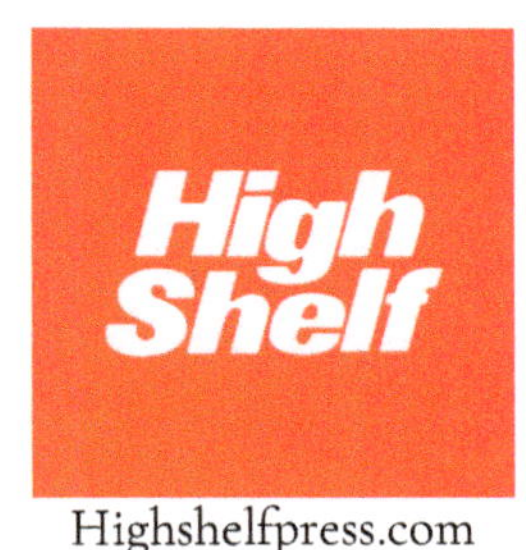